The Poetry Bl

William Matthews

The Poetry Blues

ESSAYS AND INTERVIEWS

Edited by Sebastian Matthews
and Stanley Plumly

Ann Arbor

THE UNIVERSITY OF MICHIGAN PRESS

A CIP catalog record for this book is available from the British Library.

Library of Congress Cataloging-in-Publication Data

Matthews, William, 1942– *1997*
    The poetry blues : essays and interviews / William Matthews ;
selected by Sebastian Matthews and Stanley Plumly.
        p.   cm. — (Poets on poetry)
    ISBN 0-472-09773-3 (alk. paper) — ISBN 0-472-06773-7 (pbk. :
alk. paper)
    1. Matthews, William, 1942– .—Interviews.   2. Poets,
American—20th century—Interviews.   3. Poetry—Authorship.   4.
Poetry.   I. Matthews, Sebastian, 1965–   .   II. Plumly, Stanley.   III.
Title.   IV. Series.
PS3563.A855 P64   2001
811´.54—dc21   2001000481

Editors' Notes

By definition death leaves unfinished business. For a poet much of that unfinished business is unpublished poems. For William Matthews it was also a substantial miscellany of ungathered prose—essays, commentaries, musings, interviews, and so forth—of which *The Poetry Blues* is the essential selection.

The announced subject in these pages is poetry: poetry blues, poetry and music, bad lines, sentences, durations, awkwardnesses, precision, brevity, and privacy. But the real matter, the subversive subject, is Matthews's mind, the way it subtly and irrevocably turns the collective sow's ears of questions, clichés, assignments, and analyses into singular silk purses. Matthews had the passionate intellectual capacity of a Coleridge, with the equal ability to articulate well into the night. He was also a man of diligent taste, especially with words, who could, when lost in thought, go absolutely silent. Wherever he went in those taciturn moments, he always returned with the insight and wisdom one needed. The care of the thinking and writing, the careful measure of wit and pleasure, the distances recovered from the meditations to be found here are emblematic of the heroic quality of Matthews's integrity and intelligence.

There is great heart here, too. Vigilant against pomp and hype, Matthews is in favor of good sense, good work, and the legacy that makes the contemporary possible. His sympathies are with commitment and excellence, never with reputations. And he applies the same disinterestedness to himself, which is why his interviews are so attractive and disarming. The range of his reading and knowledge is obvious—from Martial to Merwin, Cavaradossi to Mingus, lexicography to lyricism—yet it is the attitude toward the issue under discussion, Matthews's equanimity, his sense of balance toward his material, that gives his critical voice its distinction. Matthews's tone is a beautiful mixture of patrician and democrat, professional and keen amateur, practitioner and observer, uncle and wiser brother.

This is the Matthews so many of us loved in his quick takes and longer solo runs. These pages represent his word, his sweet mind, and nearly everything else we have left of him.

Stanley Plumly
Bethesda, Md.

My father died having just completed a manuscript of poems. The book, prophetically titled *After All*, was already sitting on the desk of his editor, Peter Davison. Only minor details needed to be attended to for publication, most of which were lovingly and painstakingly performed by Davison and my father's partner, Celia Bellinger.

Such was not the case with this book. In fact, I had no idea that my father might have been thinking of gathering a second collection of essays until stumbling upon a computer file labeled "Essays, 1993–1997." In it, I found a dozen or so essays and reviews, many published previously in literary magazines. There were also lying around, as you might imagine, various file folders containing old interviews and earlier essays not appearing in his first prose collection (*Curiosities* [1989]).

In among these papers and files I came across a strikingly wide variety of forms: journal entries; autobiographical sketches; remembrances; poetry reviews; essays on music, art, and the craft of writing; interviews and self-interviews; journalistic profiles; short stories; introductions and prefaces for books of translation; lecture notes; and a few short pieces that can only be called musings.

The need for a second book of "occasional prose" was obvious. The poet Stanley Plumly—not only my father's good friend but also his appointed literary executor—agreed with this conclusion, urging me to send the material along. David Lehman, the editor of the Poets on Poetry series, was enthusiastic about the project from the beginning. Before long Stan and I had narrowed the material down. The guidelines we set for choosing the work were relatively simple, with only a few casual rules.

Though a masterful and eager interviewee, Matthews often revisited themes in his interviews—jazz, the use of wit in poetry, his love of Martial and Horace—therefore, we decided to include two or three of the most succinct interviews, trusting less to represent more. Likewise, his generosity and intelligence toward fellow poets led my father to write numerous book reviews—not only reviews for friends and colleagues but also for poets of the generations preceding and following his. We would focus on reviews that (1) discussed poets prominent in Matthews's own literary and personal life (Hugo, Merwin, Kinnell, Carruth); and (2) went beyond simply reviewing a book and entered into a one-way conversation with some of his most preoccupying interests (friendship, jazz, etc.).

There were other small decisions. For example, it made sense to include some of my father's journal entries because, for all intents and purposes, he used the form the way he used the essay and the interview—as a public, therefore self-conscious, means to explore the subjects that engaged him outside the scope of, and in addition to, his poetry. For similar reasons any piece not clearly intended for publication—private journals, letters, unfinished or unformed creative or critical material—was left out.

In the end we decided on twenty-seven pieces, a good many of which were written in the last ten years, with a few going back to earlier in my father's career. The most recent piece is the interview he conducted with good friend and longtime editor Peter Davison for *Atlantic Unbound,* the *Atlantic Monthly*'s on-line poetry forum. It felt fitting to end the book in such a fraternal manner, as it did starting off the book with autobiographical pieces and remembrances of my father's old friend and mentor Richard Hugo. We'd come full circle.

Sebastian Matthews
Asheville, N.C.

Contents

The Poetry Blues

Durations

The amnesia that surrounds our earliest life is not only a great human mystery but also a receptacle into which is poured by the baby's relatives the beginnings of a life story. In later years these relatives can look at the grown child and see their first observations confirmed, for was he not always a curious baby, a cranky baby, a calm baby, what have you? We come into the world swaddled in the beginnings of a story, and, by the time we begin remembering and tending it, it already has a shape and a momentum.

When I was born, in 1942, my young parents were following my father's naval orders around the country—Bremerton, Washington; Norman, Oklahoma. I spent many of my first months with my father's parents in Cincinnati. There are photographs of me in, of course, a sailor suit. The lawn at the back, or western side, of my grandparents' house had a few huge trees—could they have been oaks?—and I think I remember standing at the edge of that lawn, on a kind of flagstone patio, in the late-afternoon light, staring excitedly and contentedly at the effect the tall trees and their long shadows made. The world seemed vast and full of comfortable mystery, and yet I was but a few feet from the safety of the house.

But that would have, of course, been later, when I was four or maybe even six. I stood there often. And, of course, I've seen photographs of the lawn and house. And maybe I'm recalling some older relative's anecdote about a boy at the edge of a lawn that somehow, inexplicably, has got blended into my own memories, like vodka slipped into a bowl of punch.

My earliest memory seems to be from the backyard of my

From the *Contemporary Authors Autobiography Series,* vol. 18 (Detroit: Gale Research, 1994).

mother's mother's house in Ames, Iowa. There's a sandbox, a tiny swatch of grainy sidewalk, and—there! it's moving—a ladybug. I have tried again and again to construct a tiny narrative from these bright props, but they won't connect. They lie there and gleam with promise but won't connect.

The war ended, my sister Susan was born, my father took a job with the Soil Conservation Service in Ohio, and then the four of us were in a boxy farmhouse outside Rosewood, Ohio, for a year and then moved into a house just outside the city limits of Troy, Ohio.

The smells of that house, that life, those years, I absorbed all unthinkingly, as greedily and easily as breath. Later, thinking back fondly on them, I at first organized them easily: indoors and outdoors, female and male.

Coffee, dishwashing liquid, baking are foremost among the kitchen smells, and the braided scent of misty heat and faint scorch that meant ironing. I remember, too, coming home from school during the Army-McCarthy hearings to find my mother ironing glumly, fascinated and appalled by what I now know to call the self-righteousness and swagger and mendacity of the whole gloomy circus. Once or twice—I think I remember this correctly—she was weeping a little. A child's world is small. Think how easily I wrote *the war ended* earlier. I don't remember it myself. In 1945 I remember I suddenly had a sister. I saw in the kitchen those puzzling afternoons how the cruelty of the official world, the world that history records and by whose accounts I knew to write that *the war ended,* could come into the house and linger, itself a sort of odor.

The kitchen held also a great terror—the pressure cooker. I must have asked about it and must have received an enthusiastically scientific description. It was like a bomb, then, I knew instantly. We were only the matter of time, the whole family, the house, perhaps the hapless neighbors. I walked past it like a paperboy skirting a sleeping Doberman. Any day it would bulge and redden and shudder and blow, and we would rise in shards and fall in flecks, and there was no help for us. How could I warn anyone? A little child shall save them, but, if that little child had waked his parents too many times to police the closet and scour the pit beneath his bed, how could he militate defense against death by pressure cooker shrapnel and broccoli? I wouldn't say a word, and when we were all dead they'd know how right I'd been in what I had not said, and they'd be sad.

The dominant outdoor and male odor was liniment: my father played for (and later, managed) a local amateur baseball team. There was the very soil of Miami County, brought home in smears and small clods on my father's boots from the farms he visited on his job. The smell of the leather of my first baseball glove and the oil I eagerly rubbed into it brings back to me not only that early proud ownership but also the odors of one of the night games my father's team played: the smell of car engines cooling in the parking lot; a little infield dirt swirling in the night air; sweat and flannel and liniment; and now and then from the stands, signaled by the sound of a church key carving triangular holes into the top of a beer can and a small sigh of released carbonation, the yeasty aroma of beer as the regular spectators settled in for a long game.

Before I started school, my mother taught me to read, and so the smell of newsprint meant to me then the eagerly awaited Sunday comics as surely as bells meant food to Pavlov's dogs. It's that smell that came first to confound the categories by which I'd later organized my olfactory memories. It's an indoor and female smell, in an obvious way, for I read the comics indoors, and I reveled as much in my mother's attention as I did in learning.

But reading leads you out of yourself as well as in and reveals, even in the comics, a world larger than home, more various than Troy, Ohio, and rewards you for the early labors of reading with the increasing knowledge that, if you can read, you hold a passport to that world. The borders between indoors and outdoors, between the largely domestic comforts of the "female" world and the harsher, more public strivings of the "male" world, come to seem thin and elastic.

My love of newsprint didn't dim. I delivered the *Dayton Daily News* in the early mornings for years and was the editor of my high school newspaper and worked two of my college summers for a small community paper in Cincinnati.

But the best thing my newspaper-boy days brought me was Spot, the dumpy dog. "Vaguely beagle," as I described her in a poem, she followed me one morning for the whole length of my route. She was waiting for me the next morning, and I was like some inexplicable canine Pied Piper, for dog after dog joined us as I covered my route. Dogs love me, I thought, but in fact, as my parents explained to me, Spot was in heat. We took her in, and slowly the blood-stirred males dispersed. She lived fifteen more years, with her faint, persistent smell, in all seasons, of leaf mold and her peculiar way of cocking her head as if someone only she could hear had made an especially apt comment. My parents let me name her, I hardly need to say, and praised me for giving her the best possible name. But one day I found my mother shooing the dog out the back door from the kitchen and murmuring to herself, with a pleased smile, "Out, out, damn Spot."

There was a basket over the garage door, and the solitude I didn't share with a dog or a pile of books from the library I spent with a basketball. These are, I now think, the imaginary friends a boy has when he is too old to admit to himself he wants an imaginary friend.

I shot baskets long into grainy dusk. I shot baskets in the rain, when the slick ball took on an orange-pink tinge and the dirt that gloved my hands and tarred my clothes came not only from the driveway but also from the specklets of dust that raindrops form around. I shoveled snow from the driveway to clear a space to shoot baskets. And now and then on Saturday afternoons, when my parents had locked themselves into their bedroom to make love, as I now know, and I could sense that they were, in any case, not thinking of me, I would shoot baskets and take care to have the ball carom off the side of the house beneath their bedroom window with its drawn shade. "Now, now," my young unconsciousness cried out, "none of that."

Troy was a company town, and the company was Hobart, makers of scales and kitchen equipment. Its visible largesse was the Hobart Arena, where Susan would go to practice her figure skating and I to play junior hockey, an activity almost as favored as youth baseball because the Arena was home to a minor league hockey team.

Susan became a dancer, a choreographer, and a respected teacher of dance at Queens College in New York City. When I moved to New York in 1983 I asked her to recommend an orthopedist to look at the knees I had gnarled from thousands of hours of driveway and playground basketball. She became, for all the years I spent on the baseball diamond and on basketball and tennis courts, the better athlete, the one who lived the possibility that the body can shape the soul as readily as vice versa. My father was a good football player and wrestler as a young man and a good catcher for that baseball team in Troy and an avid though ordinary golfer in his later years. I had neither the body nor the temperament for his sports, but as a boy baseball player I was a catcher. I didn't need to crusade for his affection; he gave it freely. I imitated him from love and admiration and because I wanted to know, I now think, something he knew about physical life. In one of those instructive ironies life so richly and relentlessly provides, my little sister, in her frilled and terraced skating costumes, was the one who learned it, and my father never played a minute's catch with her in the yard while Spot barked at the balls she failed to catch nor explained to her the Vardon grip.

I took piano lessons, but my attention slackened, and I rode my bike to the library and back, to the baseball diamond—I wore my Williams Meat Market tee-shirt proudly everywhere—and back. I mowed the neighbors' lawns for pocket money. I fell in love with unidentical twins, I corrected my fifth-grade teacher's grammar and took her just wrath broadside, I hired myself out as a boy caddy to the Hobart moguls at the local country club.

Just before we moved to Cincinnati at the start of my eighth-grade year, I took a girl, my spurned piano teacher's daughter, to the movies and then to someplace where we could get a soda or an ice cream. A couple of older boys—I'd played baseball with and against them—couldn't let a chance like this go by. "Is she your honey?" one of them asked me in a low voice just out of her hearing. Didn't I have a girl on my arm, and a beauty at that? Wasn't I a boy of the world? Wouldn't I soon be one of them? "Yes," I admitted. "Well then," he said, and his voice turned clarion, "if she's your honey, why don't you eat her?"

Something more interesting by far happened before we moved to Cincinnati. Children's International Summer Villages (CISV), a peace organization whose main project was to bring eleven-year-old children from various countries together for a summer month, decided to send a delegation to Sweden from

Miami County, and I was chosen as one of the four children who would go.

So in 1954 I spent a month outside Göteborg with kids from seven other countries, happy, curious about the cultures and habits and languages of the other children, playing games I'd never heard of before. And singing, always a hallmark of CISV gatherings, I've learned since.

We had been chosen without any expectation that our families would pay for the trip, and in order to keep the selection process democratic it was expected that a returning delegation help to raise money for the next year's. I found myself with a small slide show talking to the Lions Club, the Kiwanis, etc. My presentation, once I'd polished it a little, explained the CISV program, studded the program with a few boyish jokes, and gave thumbnail sketches of the various delegates pictured in the slides. I taught myself, without ever quite naming the project, to become an effective public speaker.

Meanwhile, my father had volunteered to do some organizational and fund-raising work for CISV and got so involved in it and so good at it that a job offer came to him. Would he run the U.S. office of CISV, located in Cincinnati, where the program had been founded?

Yes, he and Mother decided, and we were off to Cincinnati.

A last glimpse of Miami County. It's the 1952 presidential campaign, the last one to use trains for whistle-stop campaigning. Mother has decided to take me to see Adlai Stevenson and President Truman, who'd been called in to add some force to Stevenson's hopeless campaign against Eisenhower. There were few enough Democrats in the county, and few of them came out. The train stopped at a train crossing in Troy, the two principals spoke briefly, and the train chugged off. I remember a few women who had, like Mother, brought a child or two and a few campaign aides, they must have been, wearing suits and carrying clipboards or manila envelopes. Mostly the other kids, like me, were looking around and at each other. This is a little bit of history, their mothers may well have told them, too.

It was probably twenty-five years later that I found myself, for some reason, telling someone at a literary party my impressions of that day. The poet Stanley Plumly, now one of my closest friends, came across the room to tell me he'd been there that day too, from Piqua, with his mother. "I think she had a sort of crush on Stevenson," he said, "well spoken, worldly, an ironic gentleman."

"Mine, too," I said.

Mother had grown up in Missouri and Iowa. She was of Norwegian background, and there was a streak of prairie populism in her family that countered the sometimes gloomy Lutheran solipsism one could find all too easily in such communities. Her mother died not long after giving birth to her, and her father, a professor and passionate liberal, died before I ever met him. When I met her stepmother, she was running an employment agency in Lincoln, Nebraska; I think it catered mostly to women who also needed to apply a steady and routine courage to the problems of daily life. Mother came from a relatively poor family with a staunch belief in education, and the two towns where I visited my maternal grandmother were both university towns. It was in Ames, Iowa, where my parents met. Mother was an undergraduate, on scholarship. Father, a Princeton graduate, was taking a master's degree in organic chemistry to prepare him for work in agriculture.

Father's father ran a farm management company outside Cincinnati, so Father's plan to work for the Soil Conservation Service put him in the same line of work but not in business. Similarly, his first assignment put him some distance from Cincinnati but not a great distance. Many a young man fond of his parents has tried to balance that affection with his own need to break away and be on his own path, and it's hard juggling.

Also, Miami County had a high number of Amish, Mennonite, and Dunkard farmers in it; they were some of the best small farmers in America and in scant need, Father realized early, of advice on scientific farming from a recent Princeton graduate. Much of the time Father had been muddying his boots in the fields had been spent learning about farming from local experts.

The move to Cincinnati meant taking on the international focus of CISV and considerable travel. Both my parents must have been pleased and excited with this new momentum, which would carry them, in another ten years, to England, where Father ran the CISV international office for twenty years, until his retirement, and where he and Mother hosted visitors from all over the world, and from where they traveled all over the world. The promises of their separate early lives and their young marriage began to take enduring shape when they decided to move to Cincinnati.

But to Susan and me it meant terror, as all moves do at first for children. My new school had two thousand students in grades 7–12. I had the monstrous egotism of my age and imagined I was the only one of them rancid with fear. At the time, of course, I didn't think back to the pressure cooker nor think of the plots of the grade-B horror movies I loved so fiercely in those years.

In such films there's one character who knows that giant, irradiated ants are the cause of all the dead state troopers and the stink of formic acid, and everyone else thinks he's crazy. That radiation was often part of the plot, and that Japan and the United States were the two countries where almost all these films were made tells us something about the way history induces nightmares and also something about the way the manufactured nightmares of the film industry hope both to exploit and comfort our usual bad dreams, the ones with dank sweat and twisted sheets and not a whiff of popcorn.

But the terrors of those years proved negotiable. I played basketball, not with great distinction but well enough to disguise myself as a jock, which turned out to be great protective coloration for a bookish and dreamy boy. And I wasn't to be at school in Cincinnati long. I did my last three years of high school at boarding school—Berkshire School, near Great Barrington, Massachusetts. Two hundred students. In that smaller arena I edited the high school paper and the literary magazine, played basketball, collected good grades, and got myself admitted to Yale. Along the way I had some excellent instruction in English from three teachers—Thomas Chaffee, Arthur Chase, and James Durham—who sharpened considerably my skills as a reader and writer. It now began to seem possible that my dreaminess, obsessive reading, and love of words pointed toward writing or editing or teaching or some combination of the three. He was always a chatty baby, the relatives remembered.

Cleanth Brooks and John Hollander were two professors especially helpful to me. I published two poems in the *Sewanee Review* my sophomore year and married Marie Harris, herself an apprentice writer, at the end of that year. Soon enough we two literary babies had our first child, Bill. Time swirled. I graduated, and we headed for graduate school in Chapel Hill, North Carolina; Marie was due, with Sebastian, in late August, and the next week my classes would begin. We were in an apartment complex with many young couples; the stunned women, their lives transformed so rapidly and thoroughly by early motherhood, would gather around the sandbox and swings, keep an eye on their toddlers, and compare notes. The men went to classes and then came home to diapers and colic. We were around for more of domestic life than men who worked nine to five, but the distribution of labor was so vastly unequal, and discontent simmered between the sexes, all the more complicatedly in those couples where real love bound one to another.

I was trying to balance family life and my literary ambitions and uneasy about it because my work—and I could barely call it work, for I was a student—came first and my family next. Also it seemed clear to me that my work—my studies—was not what I really wanted to do. I could "do scholarship," as the idiom had it, but not with excellence or passion. What seemed to my fellow graduate students the path (*la via diretta*) to the Ph.D. degree seemed to me a dark wood (*una selva oscura*).

I had a crisis of faith. I had won a scholarship on which my family could almost live, and it had been awarded to me with every expectation that I would be avid for the Ph.D. degree. My generous parents were sending us two hundred dollars a month, not a small sum for them in those years, to make up what of our modest expenses the scholarship didn't cover; no doubt my parents had similar expectations. My wife resented—how could she not?—the way I could name an obligation and leave the house to meet it. And so I scarcely relished telling her, and so I didn't, how little that obligation truly engaged me, day by day.

And like anyone caught in a mess of his own making, I was angry.

And so I began to write poems seriously. I had written and even published a few poems when I was in college. I cared about them furiously while I was writing them, and then I was done. Now I wrote, and the poems weren't good enough, and I thought about them all the time. I was never done. It wasn't that I wrote poems because I knew that was what I really wanted to do. Indeed, I wrote poems to escape thinking about what I really wanted to do. But I wrote them as if some essential honesty in me were at stake—and I think now, as I did then, that it was—and as if writing them so seriously led me to understand that what I really wanted to do was to write poems.

I didn't want to devote the time I could spend teaching myself to write poems to writing a dissertation. Perhaps I was wrong to think of it as an either/or proposition, but I did. The dissertation was, after all, a prerequisite for a teaching job, and if I let it drift, and every day I chose to let it drift, how would I support my family?

There were jobs teaching creative writing, of course, and as luck would have it I found one, and before I reported for duty I had a book of poems accepted for publication. As well as I had woven that net of likely crisis for myself, I somehow wriggled through it.

So I was feeling pleased with myself the day Marie and the boys and I drove toward our new home and my first teaching job. I'd been to Aurora, New York, for the interview. It was a village of six hundred on the western shore of Cayuga Lake; it grew to twelve hundred when the students were in town. We drove over a brow, and there it lay below us, tiny and bucolic. My wife broke into tears.

Sebastian had responded to a new home by walking out onto the porch and surveying the territory. "Where are the friends?" he asked. He'd need to ask again in a year, as I moved from Wells College to Cornell. We were there four years. I wrote my second book. The marriage exhausted itself and collapsed. The boys were brave but hurt. They spent four school years with Marie and then came to live with me during their school years and with Marie for summers.

By then I was in Boulder, Colorado. I had a house in the mountains with two fireplaces and five acres of rocks, mountain meadowlands, and Ponderosa pines, riddled by beetles, and a dog—the ninety-five-pound, mush-hearted Underdog (you don't name a German Shepherd that size Fang). But when the boys arrived, the place came to life.

I taught there five years and then five years at the University of Washington. Bill and Sebastian both finished high school in Seattle and went to Pitzer College. Bill, a good painter, has settled in Seattle. Sebastian is currently in his last semester in the graduate program in creative writing at the University of Michigan; he's a prose writer.

When Sebastian left Seattle for college, I came to New York. I could almost write *came back,* for New York had been the preferred weekend destination from boarding school and then from college. I came for the museums and especially for the jazz clubs. I saw Monk, the great Charles Mingus, Miles Davis, Blossom Dearie, Betty Carter, Stan Getz, Ornette Coleman, John Coltrane, Eric Dolphy, Roy Eldridge, Al Cohn and Zoot Sims, Cannonball Adderly. The large world, which had beckoned to me first from reading and then from the international outlook CISV and my parents fostered in me, had one of its major crossroads in New York. It would take me a while to learn that what is most alluring about a great city is not its sophistication—this is often not much more than a huge concentration of money and goods in the social arena and a certain mandarin swagger in the arts—but the anthology of provincialisms that such a city collects. The rich linguistic pool excited me—all those languages overheard on the streets and all the dialects of English! The restaurants seemed to include every possible cuisine, and, though I couldn't afford most of them, it pleased me to think they were there, the way I had been excited on my first visits to the public library in Troy. All those books, and I might read any of them.

When I came back to New York, then, in 1984, I first taught at Brooklyn College, where I met John Ashbery's classes when he was briefly ill. I began the following year at City College, where I now hold a professorship and where a number of distinguished writers—Don Barthelme, Grace Paley, Adrienne Rich—have taught in recent years. I have now and then taught an extra course for the graduate writing program at Columbia—moonlighting, so to speak, though Columbia holds its classes in the daytime. The program's generous offer has been for me to teach a seminar of my own devising. I've taught a course in the Roman poets, including my beloved Martial; I'm finishing work this spring on a book of translations of one hundred Martial epigrams. I've taught a course called Freud for Writers and taught Virgil, Homer, and Dante. This happy arrangement has permitted me to continue my own education and provided extra dollars to spend on opera tickets and at the jazz clubs and now and then at one of those restaurants I can now sometimes afford.

The jazz clubs of my youth, with their blue coils of cigarette smoke and bad "Italian" food, are gone. The Half Note is gone, the Five Spot is gone, the Showplace on West Fourth Street where Mingus fired a dozen pianists every six months is gone. Twice I saw him harry a pianist from the stage in mid-set. This last year I saw Gerry Mulligan at the Blue Note and Tommy Flanagan, the Mozart of the jazz piano, at the Village Vanguard, and the house asked its patrons not to smoke during the performances. It's not only that smoking is avidly vilified, but it's also that Flanagan has a heart condition and Mulligan the look of a man made wary by the damage he inflicted on himself when younger. Some of the jazz buffs I sat in the clubs with in the early 1960s had in common with fans of stock car racing a secret desire to watch someone go up in flames. "He's really strung out tonight," they would say to one another. That these disaster buffs were usually white and comparatively secure materially and the musicians black and on the economic edge made this prurience all the more repulsive. Some of the use that the more flamboyant jazz musicians and abstract expressionist painters of that period offered to their audience was very nearly the use a throat offers a vampire and just as gratefully received.

In 1984 Arlene Modica and I were married in New York. Arlene was working as a publicist for Villard, a division of Random House, and then later for Putnam. You could tell from a look at her apartment that she was in publishing; all her books were hardcovers. What she hoped to do, instead, was to become a psychoanalyst and to write. She entered a psychoanalytic institute and began taking courses, and she started work on a book called, rather ominously, *Why Did I Marry You Anyhow?* Houghton Mifflin bought the book, which did well enough that there was some competition—Scribner's prevailed—to publish her next book, *If I Think About Money So Much, Why Can't I Figure It Out?* (1991). As things turned out, the marriage was brief. We had both witnessed vitriolic and expensive divorces and promised each other to do better. No such parting is truly amicable, but we kept our promises. Today Arlene is a practicing analyst, a proven author; she's remarried happily and expecting, as I write, her first child.

In 1989 my father died. My parents had been in the States, and I'd scheduled a book party for *Blues if You Want* during their visit, so they could attend. The next day they flew back to England, and my father had a massive heart attack at the luggage retrieval area in the Newcastle upon Tyne airport. He was sixty-nine.

Susan and I flew to England to help Mother with the funeral. My father's father had died when I was in my early twenties; it was the first death that shook me at my center. In the intervening years I've seen the deaths of writers and musicians who'd meant as much to me as family members—Thelonious Monk, Charles Mingus, Vladimir Nabokov, Elizabeth Bishop. In the case of artists like these, whose continued development and invention had produced not only beloved work but a model for the way a life in the arts can be imagined and lived out, the deaths meant an absolute end to the marvelous momentum by which an important body of work is produced. Here were people who seemed able to bring the whole weight of their lives to bear on the next poem or novel or performance, and suddenly that weight was airy nothing.

I felt it again with writers I had some friendship with—James Wright, Richard Blessing. Richard Hugo's death meant the loss of a good friend and one of my favorite poets. It began to feel to me that we spent the first half of our lives saying hello, slowly working our way from the isolations and narcissisms of childhood into a larger world, only to spend the second half of our lives saying good-bye. "Death," Wallace Stevens wrote, "is the mother of beauty." When I was younger, the fluent ease with which the Twenty-Third Psalm refers to the span of our lives as "the valley of the shadow of death" seemed to me a great rhetorical flourish; I now think it an achievement of exemplary accuracy.

A world in which I cannot share another meal with my father is a diminished one, but the young can fill some of these holes with their expanding presences. The love of a parent and child is the only central love in our lives whose goal is some large measure of separation, and my sons, each in his late twenties, are busy building some autonomy in their lives. All the same, we're in frequent and affectionate communication. Watching them try to build lives in the arts has been a great pleasure to me.

Bill and Rochelle have provided me a grandchild, Raven William, the behemoth baby (twenty-five pounds at nine months). And I think of myself as an honorary grandfather to Rochelle's daughters from an early marriage, Alison and Davey.

Other compensations from the young have come from many of my students. A pleasingly large number of them have gone on from their student days to make lives as writers and, frequently, as teachers, too. Their devotion to a difficult craft in a culture that has marginalized poetry speaks well for the rewards of writing; these are seldom worldly rewards, to be sure, but the private and interior ones are great. And of course there's a crucial stewardship these writers and teachers perform for a society that doesn't know enough to value it: the work of exploring and maintaining the mysterious link between our language and our emotional lives.

But the largest compensation is the tang of mortal fear. I have never been more aware that the meter is running and, consequently, never been more vivid, concentrated, happy, or warily hopeful.

How might I better embody such cautious optimism than to marry a third time?

Of course, the vows, as we pronounced them before Nathaniel Dean, attorney general of the Bahamas, in Nassau, in early December 1989, said nothing about "cautious optimism" and didn't include Dr. Johnson's famous jape about "the triumph of hope over experience" and didn't allude to Chekhov's wry observation that if you are afraid of loneliness you shouldn't marry. They don't quote Chaucer on "the woe that is in marriage" or mention Madame Bovary, and they were written long before Thurber made his heartbroken jokes and strangled cartoons about the war between the sexes. Jane Austen was not quoted nor Emily Dickinson:

> To make a prairie it takes a clover and one bee,
> One clover, and a bee,
> And revery.
> The revery alone will do,
> If bees are few.

Nor was Simone de Beauvoir mentioned.

We were asked, and we had volunteered to be asked, Patricia and I, to say the time-honored and time-abused vows, properly rinsed by feminism of the verb *obey* and other like anachronisms.

We had planned our trip and worked out the bureaucratic details—it was my third marriage and Pat's second, so there was plenty of paperwork—by phone with Mr. Dean's office. And then my father died three weeks before the date we'd set. We'd keep the date, we decided, for what else could it mean to say the words "for better or for worse"? So Pat, in the dress we'd bought the day before, and I in my white suit wrinkled from being packed, or wrinkled from being worn on the plane to keep it from being wrinkled by being packed, I can't remember which, stood in Nathaniel Dean's office and were married. Pat is a writer and teacher and a beauty in body and soul, a mother of three whose lives I'm happy to be entangled in, and the best of companions.

I like to think of myself as by nature a domestic person. I cooked for and made a home for my sons for their junior high school and high school years, in addition to the usual fatherly activities. I'm a reader, a listener to music, a man made happy by kitchen chores and pleased when there are friends at my table. My marital history casts a considerable shadow on this sunny portrait.

It's also true that I have had thirteen domiciles—thirteen sets of change of address notices mailed, thirteen massive packings and unpackings of books, thirteen new phone numbers, etc.—since I was first married. How many blenders, extension cords, clay pots for the new houseplants I'd bought, etc., have I bought in ritual tribute to the gods of restlessness? I do not count summer rentals, the sparse comforts of the rooms given to the faculties of summer writers' conferences, writers' colonies, hotel rooms. I only count the ones that counted, and they are thirteen.

Soon it will be ten years that I have lived in New York (three addresses). Already I have been at one address for a record length of time and taught at the same university for a record length of time. I have finally found a home, I could say with a self-dramatizing flourish. But that would be morally melodramatic and would obscure a couple of important truths.

One is that I found a way to be at home wherever I lived and taught, with the exception of Seattle and the University of Washington. In those years first Bill and then Sebastian left home for college, and I found myself depressed, more deeply rootless than I'd ever admitted to myself, and ricocheting around like a squash ball. I had, like many a parent, described my life as organized around and given over to my children, and, when the ordinary maturation of the boys made that explanation of myself an occasional rather than a daily motto, I had to begin admitting how poorly I knew me. What did I want? I had almost no idea.

The other is that I have loved restlessness and seen in it and in its most reputable manifestation, travel, a vivid metaphor for curiosity. I have been around because I wanted to go around. I whirled my bike to the Troy, Ohio, library, hoping to be transported, and it worked. Around the world in eighty books, or eighty thousand.

What I want now is to make for that restless imagination a durable home. Hasn't it done as much for me?

Instrumental Bones

Interview with Dave Johnson

What was your evolution in the arts? Which came first, poetry or music?

I was an early reader—my mother taught me. But music came first. We have rhythm before we have discourse. And while there's a long musical tradition of prepubescent prodigies, poets are usually very long in the making.

Why do you think that is?

I don't know. Neither poetry nor music is easy.

Perhaps there's some part of the brain where related skills— math, music, and chess—get learned that can produce, on the short side of puberty, work that's extraordinary by adult standards. I'm thinking not only of child prodigy instrumentalists but of childhood compositions by Mozart and Rossini, let's say, that have not only survived but move and engage us.

Poets are turtles: not Keats, not Rimbaud, but most poets.

Theoretical physicists, I'm told, are assumed to be past their peak by their mid-thirties. A dancer my age is a choreographer or an ex-dancer. The vocal chords and the rest of a singer's equipment start slowly deteriorating in that singer's late twenties, but very slowly, so disciplined singers can grow smarter faster than they tatter and thus have very long careers.

But in their forties and fifties and sixties our best poets outdo and outdo themselves.

Is this because the psyche builds on itself in some way? A foundation gets laid and then . . .

Look at a representative anthology of younger poets published long enough ago that we've got some retrospect. Daniel Halpern's *The American Poetry Anthology* (1976) will serve. There

From *High Plains Literary Review* (1995).

are of course exclusions that seem inexplicable now (what? no Robert Morgan poems?). Bouquets fade, and *anthology* comes from a Greek word that means something close to *bouquet.* But Halpern's is a very good anthology.

These young poets are laying foundations. And it looks as though they're all building similar houses. No, I should say not *they* but *we,* for I'm in that book. It looks like we're all building similar houses. Young poets have a common pool of subject matter: childhood, early confrontations with mortality, the passage into adult sexuality, etc. The poems that result from swimming in this pool have kinship markings.

But open a new book by James Merrill, Adrienne Rich, or W. S. Merwin, to name some acknowledged masters, and you find poems that no other person in the gene pool could have written.

The foundation seems to be somewhat communal, and of course young poets learn by writing at least partially like other poets.

Once the foundation is down, the job seems to be to write less and less like others and more and more like yourself.

It's like building a house by yourself—satisfying but very slow work.

How have music and poetry evolved since your initial experience with each art form?

Poetry has competition it didn't have a hundred years ago, when home entertainment, as the phrase now goes, meant reading or something to do with a piano. I'm delighted, as you can see, to live in an era of recorded music.

The quality of sound is unbelievable.

Yeah, and the preservation of performances is a welcome miracle. What it means is that many an evening I might choose not to read poetry. There are also videocassettes and even television itself, a usually dingy but not Satanic medium. There's a lot of worthy competition for people's attention.

Especially in a place like New York.

Exactly.

You look at the New York poetry calendar, and you see poetry and performance pieces and other things going on. Just making that choice seems almost impossible to do.

There must be twelve to fifteen nights a year when, in effect, Phil Levine is reading one place and Adrienne Rich another.

Did you get a chance to see them together the other night?

No, I didn't.

I didn't, either.

There you have it.

I was reading the Anita O'Day piece in your book of essays, Curiosities *(1989). You were at the Newport Jazz Festival, and she was waiting to go on stage, and you were just a kid, talking with her and lighting her cigarette. That was really a great moment.*

Michael Ondaatje, Russell Banks, and David Young put together a book of such encounters, called *Brushes with Greatness* (1989). They're all stories about meeting famous or exemplary people. Almost all of them happen during or within haling distance of adolescence; it's a book of instances of one kind of initiation rite.

It sounds like a great read. How old was Anita when you met her? Tell us a little about it.

This was 1957, or '56, I'm not sure which. We could figure this out. There was a film shot at Newport that year called *Jazz on a Summer Day*. She's in it. She most have been in her late thirties, maybe forty. She still performs and records. She has a record company called Emily, named, I think, after her cat. (He strokes the kitten's head. She has presented herself, as if on cue.)

[Laughter.] *This is great. These recordings, are they singles?*

No, whole albums. She doesn't tour but makes an occasional club appearance and records.

Where is she living?

In Connecticut, I believe. She had obviously gone out on the big band circuit as a very young woman, maybe in her late teens. That summer at Newport she was waiting around for other acts to get on and offstage; she had an hour or so to kill. She was drinking coffee and smoking and asked for a light for a cigarette.

And you were how old?

I would have been fifteen in 1957. . . .

That's pretty young to have a taste for jazz.

Well, music forms a screen between yourself and those parts of the world that you would like to keep at a distance. This is a usual teenager's use for music. But the music came to interest me more as itself than as a buffer.

Of course, I listened to the pop music of the day, which wasn't always rock 'n' roll. You could hear the real thing on "race" stations. Cincinnati had a good black station, and at night we could pick up WLAC from Nashville.

You guys could pick that up in Ohio?

Yeah. Rhythm 'n' blues, race records . . .

Blues?

Yeah, some blues. There were labels that were the black equivalents of Sun Records in Memphis. Chess Records, Checkers Records, and others. They tended to be a little farther north—Chicago, Cincinnati, here and there. There were radio stations that played this stuff, a whole night club circuit, a whole economy for this black music.

Also I listened to classical music, particularly Bach. And lots of jazz. Reading and listening to music were respected activities in our household.

Did you study music when you were young?

I took piano lessons in my early grade school years and clarinet lessons later on. I studied with a guy who was first clarinet for the Cincinnati Symphony Orchestra. He was a far better teacher than I was a student.

My fantasy was that I'd learn to play the clarinet, which is technically harder than a saxophone, and then I'd master the sax family and "have a career in music."

But I had less aptitude than I'd hoped, and so my career would, realistically, have meant weddings, bar mitzvahs, the occasional bar gig. Or, in another likely outcome, years of teaching students as indifferent as I rapidly became.

To the extent that I was looking ahead—much of what I'm describing here is hindsight—I was mistaken. Most of what fuels you when you're learning a complicated skill is the pleasure of learning itself. You build from what you learn, and then you learn a next thing and a next. You're also learning, though it will be awhile before you realize this, a reverence for the skill itself, its difficulty, its intricacy, its power. These rewards would in themselves have been quite enough, dreamy adolescent considerations of a great career aside.

But I didn't learn well enough or fast enough to provide myself those rewards, and thus I stopped.

A good chess player can look at the board and sense that his knight is in trouble "soon." If you stop to analyze the sequence of moves that will make that trouble material, you'd find how many they are. Let's say seven. As a musician, I was, when I stopped, equivalent to a chess player who had to work out all seven moves logically in his head. I'd never learned to see the board.

The pleasures of the kind of learning I'm describing here are so great that I'd not be surprised to learn someday that brain research had discovered and named the little rewards secreted by the brain to seduce the brain owner away from lassitude.

Did learning to write poems hold that kind of excitement for you?

I wrote clumsily and wrote many bad poems, of course, but it was rewarding from the beginning. Perhaps the little secretions are mildly addictive. Also, I was enough older than that dreamy boy with his clarinet that I imagined no greater reward for writing poems than the continued desire to write them.

My musical career has found its exact best form, I think. I'm a habitual and greedy music consumer. Living in New York means I can go to the jazz clubs and the opera, and I spend a lot of time listening to recordings.

I didn't have to spend a life as a mediocre (or worse) musician just to prove a point. What that point would have been I have no idea.

It seems we might reach such a point with many things in our lives. Sad.

Instructive, too. I had delusions of grandeur about playing basketball when I was young. Two things helped me outgrow them. One was that the rate at which I got better started to flatten out. Two was that I hit serious competition and got humbled. I would never be better than competent, and I was ruining my knees five hours a day. That clear appraisal was sad but also a gift.

My musical fantasy involved an audience, and my basketball fantasy involved competition.

A possible life writing poems was about me alone at a desk and excited to be working. This shift in emphasis announced a willingness to try maturity.

Poetry and music seem close enough there might be some crossover.

There's something I know about phrasing and how to keep a fairly long sentence afloat for seven to a dozen lines of free verse without it losing its shape or momentum. If I'm right in thinking I can do that, I learned it more from listening to music than from listening to poetry.

How would you say that worked? What did listening to music teach you? And do you think this is a result of recorded music being more accessible than recorded poetry?

When I said "listening to poetry," I was being metaphorical; I meant the way you hear a line in your head when you read. As for your first two questions, I don't know how it works but that it works. By *it* I mean the transfer of some way of hearing music to some way of hearing the possibilities for writing a passage in a poem I'm working on. It's doubtless something I learned without being quite aware I'd learned it, a way of hearing what might happen, what's not quite available yet. This sounds, I know, as if I'm talking about improvisation, and, if there were a kind of saint attending the procedure, it might well be, in one instance, Saint Thelonious, but on other occasions it's Haydn or Verdi.

Poets write with lots of beloved poetry in their heads, passages that matter to them, and give us the true illusion that we're not writing in utter solitude. Thus my reference to saints, for these beloved passages and the poets who wrote them work for us the way the saints work in folk Catholicism, as intermediaries between us and our invisible audience and as intermediaries between the impossibility of the job we've undertaken and the completion and fullness we nonetheless hope for.

What I'm reporting is that for me sometimes those saints are musicians or composers or scraps of their music.

Do you think this comes at an early age?

I think it began at an early age, when I started listening hard to singers and horn players. In recent years I've listened as carefully to piano players.

Players in particular?

Tommy Flanagan, our greatest living jazz pianist, who has been well and frequently recorded in recent years. Also he does five or six gigs a year in New York.

Among the masters: Monk, Bud Powell, Art Tatum, and let's not forget Earl Hines. Basie was a monster pianist with delicacy to match, but his playing gets overlooked because of his sparing solos and because his contributions to jazz history are in several areas. What they all have in common, and which the next-best pianists nearly all lack, is an antic sensibility, something like a sense of humor.

Phrasing on the piano is a different matter from singing or horn playing because it's not dependent on breath.

When you read reviews of classical singing by critics lavish with jargon, you'll run across the phrase *breath control.* It doesn't refer to who can stay underwater longest but to making, during the singing of a musical passage, a steady stream of right decisions about exactly how much breath to spend on each of the steps required to get from the beginning of the passage to the end. In great singing good taste, technique and emotional expressivity become the same thing: the fountain of breath on which the song is borne aloft.

So jazz singing and horn playing suggest some likely parallels with the way well-written poems move.

As I said, the matter is more complicated when we're talking about piano playing. We'll talk about this when I've put in a few more years of listening, and maybe I'll know more to say.

How does all this relate to the measurement of a line in poetry?

The better parallel is the phrase or the sentence. The line is like the bar in music. One composes by the phrase. The bar is a useful tool for musical notation and analysis, but, like the foot in prosody, it doesn't occur in nature.

Composing by the line is like translating by the line. You're staring at the snake's belly and can't see the head or tail. You have to have the whole unit in your attention, and it's not the line but the phrase or clause or sentence.

Obviously enough, when Alexander Pope was on, his unit of attention was nearly exactly the heroic couplet. But that's a rare and splendid instance in English language poetry.

A more germane instance for recent poetry is Marianne Moore. Did she compose by the line?

The line is important but as a kind of undertow special to poetry. The surf is the syntactical unit.

Syntactical, meaning prepositional phrases, clauses, etc.?

In Janet Malcolm's *The Impossible Profession,* a book about psychoanalysts, there's a shrink who says something to the effect that sooner or later, in analysis, time comes to talk about genitals. Sooner or later, in talking about poetry, time comes to talk about grammar and syntax. Which may be why so many creative writing classes prefer to talk about the line.

One of the melodies in poetry, as in prose, is how the statement is shaped, articulated, put together. In poetry the line can sing various countermelodies.

When you write, do you work in prose and trim back?

No, I've never done that.

You work with a line structure.

Well, they come out in lines. For me the line, even if I've decided very early in writing the poem that the line is rather like a blank verse line, is the contradictory by-product of a larger unit of attention. It's not that I don't pay attention to the line but that my attention is polyphonal. The contradictory and the dictory need each other for poetry to happen.

Say you're working at a sonnet. Do you begin with form or content?

You don't have to commit the poem to a possible future as a sonnet until the thirtieth syllable, after all, in an *abab* quatrain or in *abba*. You could sit down and say to yourself, "I shall write a sonnet this day," but why wouldn't you allow yourself the benefit of all the information the writing of the first two or three lines, including the likelihood of a false start or two, can provide?

I know I'm not answering your question directly, because I can't. When I begin, I don't know what either form or content is going to be, and I'd like to maintain the benefits of that ignorance as long as possible. After all, do I really want to write something I already know or, worse, something I think I'd like to know?

One summer Carol Frost and I taught together at Bread Loaf, and she brought to class the drafts of Elizabeth Bishop's "One Art," for my money the best villanelle in English. It didn't begin as a villanelle. She tried this, she tried that, and at some point she tried a villanelle and found the right amount of resistance (I'm thinking of ohms) and completed the circuit.

I make formal decisions similarly, though not, needless to say, at the same level of success.

How would you say the musicality of a poem is affected by the psyche of the poet at different times in the poet's life? Is it a conscious choice?

How many choices are wholly conscious? But the collaboration of conscious and unconscious choices are central to writing.

As for correspondences between formal effects in poems and the poet's psyche at the time of writing the poem, there are two obvious things to say. (1) There's bound to be a connection. (2) It's impossible to "prove" such a connection.

In Roethke's late free verse poems there's a recurring device: a three- to five-line stanza, each line shorter than the one above to provide a kind of diminuendo. These passages routinely treat images of light, breath, and rest, all themes considerably braided together in the poems of this period.

We could say the formal device served as a leitmotif for those themes, for that cluster of images. But does the theme "cause" the device? Vice versa? How much choice accounts for the pairing of theme and device? How much habit?

We can say that the device and the theme frequently appear together in these late poems, but, if we then grow ambitious to prove a connection or show how it works, we run up against the considerable limits of discursive prose in describing the creative process.

A similar problem grows from the useful pun *body of work*. Mustn't form and physiology be connected? We run into the same problem. There's bound to be a connection, but we start sounding foolish when we insist on it.

Now and then someone argues that iambic is the normative meter in English poetry because it imitates the heartbeat. But French people have hearts but don't have accentual poetry.

And, of course, the relationship between poetry and music that we keep nearing and falling back from is similar. We know it's there. But, if we insist on explaining it, we run into embarrassments.

There are stories about the relationship between poetry and music, like the Orpheus story, that are utterly convincing.

And what does that suggest?

Some imaginative truths can't be proved or disproved.

What did you read when you were young?

I was a slut reader: everything. I read all the Hardy Boys books. I didn't like the first one that much, and they're all the same. What seemed to have mattered to me for a while was the possibility that I could read every book in the Troy, Ohio, public library. When I realized there were books I didn't want to read, I was both relieved and obscurely saddened. By reading I made some connection to myself and at the same time to the world that was so important that the book in hand mattered less than these connections.

At a later stage the pleasures of discrimination proved every bit as intense.

The first poet I read intensely and thoroughly was Auden. Then I read all his prose—introductions to anthologies, reviews, essays. There's a lot. For about a year I made my reading list from Auden. He wrote about *x*, I read *x*.

Did you ever meet him?

Once. I took a course at Yale called the History of the Lyric, taught by John Hollander. Two semesters. You started with Pindar in translation and were supposed to collapse in a heap in the middle of the twentieth century late in April. Rumor had it that the course was brilliant and never got out of the nineteenth century.

Hollander sometimes missed a class, and there was an unwritten rule that after you'd waited twenty minutes for a professor you could leave, and, even if he or she showed up, it didn't count as an absence.

It was an undergraduate seminar. There were about twelve of us. One day fifteen minutes had gone by, and we began to eye one another. Who'd leave first? And then Hollander came through the door with Auden, who was editing the Yale Younger Poets Prize in those years and was in town to read manuscripts. He talked to us about songs in Shakespeare's plays for an hour and a half. No notes, of course. The talk seemed to ramble, but it had a sensible shape to it. He wasn't lecturing us but thinking out loud.

Those years were the twilight of the New Criticism, and of course both Brooks and Warren taught at Yale. There was a tendency to read Shakespeare's plays as long lyric poems. Auden talked about them as plays. Where on stage should this song from that play be sung? What should the other actors be doing during the song? His talk was full of revelations.

You had read all his work before he came that day?

I had.

That's very fortunate.

Well, it's partly the read-all-the-Hardy-Boys-books-even-though-your-fillings-melt-from-boredom syndrome but expended on very worthy books.

In those years, whenever a new book by Nabokov or Auden came out, I was at the book store. A few writers become, or their books do, major characters in one's life.

True. Or musicians. In your poems about Coleman Hawkins and John Coltrane we can obviously see that it really hit you when they died. What was your relationship with them?

I loved their music so much that their deaths were real losses to me. They were heroic figures to me—who but heroes could have made such music?—and so were almost like fictional characters, who can die (Hector dies, Achilles dies) on the page but remain powerful in the imagination.

When those guys died, I thought how I'd never hear the music they'd have made if they'd lived longer, and at that selfish moment death became real to me. I didn't get it when my great-grandmother died and my great-aunt, and I obviously hadn't got it when I read *The Iliad,* but when Hawkins died, 1968, the floor opened, and it got me.

After that, when I could, I went to hear the aging masters. I heard Lester Young, not long before he died, and he was ill and tattered. But I'm glad I went.

Where was this?

He came to Cincinnati with Jazz at the Philharmonic, a kind of touring all-star jam session that Norman Granz, who ran Verve records, took around the country to prestigious theater sites: the Schubert in Cincinnati, the Opera House in Chicago, the Shrine in L.A.

There might be two trumpet players, three or four sax players, a trombonist, and a rhythm section. They played standards, and everyone soloed. Young's tone was frayed at the edges, and most of what he played he could have phoned in. But twice during the evening he played short passages (four bars?) that were phrased so elegantly nobody else could have played them.

He was dead not long after that night. My sense of loss was personal and greedy; I wanted more music.

When Nabokov died, or Bishop, I had the same piqued, acquisitive disappointment: there'd be no more new work now.

Did you ever meet Nabokov?

No. Another one-way relationship.

Even when you don't know the person, you're aware that behind the body of work there's a story.

In an earlier era of jazz slang you criticized a player with great chops but too little heart, something like this: "Yeah, he can play all over that horn, but he's got no story to tell." Music isn't narrative, so what does that mean? I think "the story" is like a well in which your accumulated emotional experience is stored, and you make a soulful solo by bringing up a ladleful so that the notes you play are wet with it.

In the case of an artist you don't know, you of course don't know his or her story, but you can sense that there is one. That's what the jazz guys meant.

Who was the best at that?

Armstrong in his era. His Hot 5 and Hot 7 solos are both full of emotion and very elegantly shaped. Coleman Hawkins, Lester Young, Ben Webster on ballads, Dizzy Gillespie, Charlie Parker, Monk, Coltrane, Rollins.

Young was the Donald Barthelme of saxophone storytellers. The work is elliptical, funny, smart, blithe surfaced, and end-lessly sad.

I was reading the essay on Stanley Plumly in Curiosities, *and was intrigued when you were discussing Plumly's poem "The Iron Lung" and said, "One way to describe the contrast between such poems and more conventionally made poems in Plumly's books is by analogy, referring to the era in jazz history when improvisations began to be based more on chord changes than on melody. The effect is that the structure and the surface of the song are no longer easy to distinguish. The music seems to be about, to the extent that music is about anything, its own shaping principles."*

That's the onset of bebop, that shift. Before then chord changes were like a stud in a wall: it's there, and you don't think about it. But why wouldn't an artisan think about his materials and make melodic use of the structure?

At that stage in Stan's work his books would have three or four big poems—big in what they could include—that were not only about boyhood but about the workings of memory as well. Those poems spurred that analogy.

You mean to be able to see the structure and then walk out of it?

Not exactly. "The Iron Lung" is not a narrative.

I have a tendency to forget that because I have heard him read it with a bit of explanation before it.

Yes. If somebody had told a narrative about being a boy in Ohio, going through the polio scare, your mother taking you to school on a Saturday to take the sugar cubes, first this, then that, what might stand out from the narrative, to an attentive listener, would be four or five highly charged and evocative details.

It's as if Stan put his poem together by taking those four or five details, discarding the entire remainder of the narrative, and building a structure that would contain those four or five details, that is, the poem. The relationship of the details to each other is metaphorical, textural, tonal, but not narrative. The poem discovers that relationship and finally is more fully about that relationship than about the iron lung or the polio scare or the boy.

The narrative impulse here corresponds to melody and the discovered relationship to chord changes. Maybe it's more ingenious than illuminating.

No, I think it works. It caught my eye because I am a fan of Plumly's work and especially that book (Out of the Body Travel). *I just wanted to hear you expound on it a little more.*

It's a beautiful poem.

I remember the time well. The fear of polio was electric.

About the same time, a kid in my class got trichinosis from undercooked pork. His mother was stigmatized. People spoke of her as if she'd poisoned him. His family grew pigs, why the hell couldn't she cook pork right?

There were things in the world you might ordinarily take in, like pork or air with a virus in it, that could make you ill, maybe crippled. It was the job of your parents to filter the poisons. The world looked beautiful, but it could be very hostile, and they were your shepherds.

The way people talked about that poor kid's poor mother meant she didn't know her job, but they knew theirs.

Just burn the pork.

Exactly. Such fears are so powerful they have to find expression opportunistically.

When I saw the movie *Alien,* in which monsters attack us from inside our bodies, I was moved and shocked—good special effects, good lurid filmmaking. Only later did I think of today's great fears: AIDS and cancer.

When we went for sugar cubes in Troy, I remember, we were so clean we almost had washcloth prints on our young skin. Our mothers nearly rubbed us raw getting the world's grime off.

Where were you living then? Troy?

Troy, Ohio. Farm country, north of Dayton. Pig and corn country, soybeans making a first inroad in the 1950s.

What did mom and dad do?

My father was the county agent for the Soil Conservation Service, a division of the Department of Agriculture. My mother had two small kids and stayed home with us. She taught me to read before I was old enough for school and encouraged me toward piano lessons later on. She encouraged my sister, who became a dancer and choreographer, to take figure skating lessons. The home she stayed in with us was no fortress but part of the large world.

How about religious background?

The signal came in faintly. In my grandfather's generation there were three daughters. Two became Episcopalian nuns. The third never married, served as a nurse and companion to her ailing mother, and did a lot of lay work for "the church," as I heard her say when I was very young.

The men in that generation went dutifully to church, an hour or two on Sunday.

Perhaps the difference between that generation and mine has less to do with religious fervor than with the greatly expanded range of what women can do with their lives.

My parents took my sister and me to church when we were young, and we dragged our tiny feet. They gave up for the best reason: their hearts weren't in it.

Miami County, of which Troy was the county seat, had a number of Mennonite and Dunkard farmers, and I went to school with their kids, whose religion lasted seven days a week. It was interesting to be around people for whom religious matters were matter-of-factly central.

But it stopped there?

It was not for me.

I was in the same classes with a Dunkard kid, probably the most intelligent human I've ever been around. His sect prohibited schooling past the eighth grade, and I thought I could see light dim in his eyes as he drew near. He was either going to stay around Troy and try to find a way not to feel starved, or he'd have to blow everything up to have an alternative. That seemed a lot of pressure on someone so young. I don't know what happened to him, doubtless because I haven't wanted to know.

Another family I knew well were Amish. The mother wore the bonnet, but the father used farm machines, which the hardliners considered wrong. The kids were all sweet-tempered and very bright, and they've all left and taken very worldly jobs—psychiatry, computers. The parents didn't lock the kids in. And so, of course, they left. Their parents were smart and humane and knew what would happen.

In a new poem about Thelonious Monk you talk a little about that.

The poem's in my oncoming book. The title is the name of a Monk composition.

Well, You Needn't

Rather than hold his hands properly
arched off the keys, like cats
with their backs up,
Monk, playing block chords,
hit the keys with his fingertips well
above his wrists,

shoulders up, wrists down, scarce
room for a pencil, ground
freshly to a point,
piano teachers love to poke
into the palms of junior
pianists with lazy hands.

What easy villains these robotic
dullards are in their floral-
print teaching dresses
(can those mauve blurs be
peonies?). The teachers' plucky
make-do wardrobes suggest, like the wan

bloom of dust the couch exhaled
when I scrunched down to wait
for Mrs. Oxley, just how we value
them. She'd launch my predecessor
home and drink some lemonade,
then free me from the couch.

The wisdom in Rocky Mount,
North Carolina, where Monk grew up,
is that those names, Thelonious
Sphere, came later, but nobody's
sure: he made his escape
by turning himself into a genius

in broad daylight while nobody
watched. Just a weird little black
kid one day and next thing anybody
knew he was inexplicable
and gone. We don't give lessons
in that. In fact it's to stave off

such desertions that we pay
for lessons. It works for a while.
Think of all the time we spend
thinking about our kids.
It's Mrs. Oxley, the frump
with a metronome, and Mr. Mote,

the bad teacher and secret weeper,
we might think on, and everyone
we pay to tend our young, opaque
and truculent and terrified,
not yet ready to replace us,
or escape us, if that be the work.

That's an interesting poem.

The securities of family life might well seem like suffocation
to a really skillful and obsessed child, until the piano becomes
his new family. For that matter, most families that have spawned
a writer have mixed feelings about it. The kid might one day
blow the whistle.

Oh, man.

I have a postcard with a photograph, taken by Jonathan
Williams, of the house where Monk grew up, on Red Row in
Rocky Mount. A dreadful shack. Williams cropped the photo so
that the house sits off to the right side, and the center of the
photograph is the road to it and away.

*You underscore the environmental hurdles a writer or musician might
face when you talk about getting away.*

Red Row's a good place to leave, I suppose, but James Mer-
rill, in his memoir, *A Different Person,* makes it eloquently clear
how he had to get away.

Such escapes are illusory, at first. Here's a passage from Her-
aclitus: "All men are deceived by the appearances of things,
even Homer himself, who was the wisest man in Greece; for he

was deceived by boys catching lice: they said to him, 'What we have caught and what we have killed we have left behind, but what has escaped us we bring with us.'"

You go away to begin to know which lice are which.

It seems to me characteristic of your imagination to find a bodily metaphor. Are the bones and the body instruments for you in some way, in your body of work?

You're talking to somebody who could, with the help of his insurers, support a small orthopedic clinic quite comfortably. Some of my interest in bones starts with the fact that some of mine don't work and remind me daily. This is so obvious it would be a mistake not to say it.

In your Coleman Hawkins poem you say, "as if that sax were made of bone wrenched from his wrist." And in "Jealousy," "If I rasp like a crashing plane, / like a ground down spine / made into a rhythm instrument, / it is because I am knitting / a fern of bone for your thigh."

Both poems are from my first book. I wrote rather more floridly then than now; I'm not sure the second passage you quoted entirely makes sense. But I see what you're pointing to.

What more can you say about it?

Well, let's take some puns that are in plain view.

Sure.

Writers are articulate; bones are articulated. Maybe the bones are the "units of attention" for the skeleton. The trombone has been nicknamed "the bone." In this instance a visual pun underwrites the linguistic one. The reason a harpsichord or fortepiano or piano keyboard looks like a squared-off set of teeth has got more to do with octaves and design problems than with our unconscious imagination, but maybe we make machines in our own image when the design exigencies permit. Drums have skins. Hearts and trumpets have valves. Stringed instruments have their own vocal cords.

Bones? We're aware we've got lymph nodes, marrow, salivary glands, etc., but no child dresses as a pancreas for Halloween. When the ashes have gone to ashes and the dust to dust, the bones remain.

Once I went to hear Willie Ruff and Dwike Mitchell perform at Mercer College, in Macon, Georgia. Ruff plays bass and French horn, and Mitchell's a monster pianist. Ruff teaches music at

Yale, and their specialty is an informal concert with commentary by Ruff. It was time to go on, and Mitchell hadn't showed, so Ruff came on and talked. He talked about his first instruments. He popped his mouth with his finger. He drummed on his chest. He played the hambone (the thigh). He snapped his fingers. It all started with my body, he was saying, because I was black and poor and that was all I had until I had an instrument, but I didn't forget.

Then there were questions and answers, and because he'd talked frankly about race and class, someone used the word *deprivation.*

He made a flurry of rhythms with his body and asked, "Is this deprivation?" There were people in the audience who, when they were restless, tuned in to CNN.

Then Mitchell showed up, emitting wisps of steam. He'd had a battle with some rental car agency, and it had racial implications. They played a furious twenty minutes and were gone.

Is the body the space from which all instruments come?

How many hands high is a horse? What are the dimensions of your rug in feet? Etc. It's not just music. Frank Lloyd Wright used to sell his clients furniture, if they'd buy it, as well as his design for the house. He was quite short, as his clients remembered when they sat in his chairs. The body is a natural measure.

But to play an instrument you have to inhabit it, animate it, haunt it, if you will, the way God haunted the waters in Genesis.

Your Coleman Hawkins poem compares muscles to rivers.

It's a central trope of love poetry that the surface of the beloved's body is like a landscape.

But what about the interior? Take one's own. The stomach gurgles, the bowels move, muscles twinge. It's a metropolis in there. And there are underground rivers. Much of the music of the interior body goes on without our instigation, the way the stairs in an old house creak, though no one's on them.

We speak of music that makes us want to dance, or want to cry—to make, in other words, voluntary and welcome some of what goes on all the time, all unheeded.

Excuse the pun, but if we can put the body together here . . . if the bones are instruments . . .

Let's say they're instrumental.

And the muscles . . . ?

Well, the muscles are like the hammers on a keyboard instrument, the valves on a horn, etc. We use our muscles to energize those muscles. (We turn the tape over and check it: recording a minute and then playing that minute back.)

But think of yourself singing in the shower. What for? For the pleasure of using your singing muscles.

And you hear what the operatic tenor Alfredo Kraus calls the "mixed voice," a combination of the inside and outside voices. The inside voice is in the resonating chamber of the body. The outside voice is what everyone else hears, but you can't, because you hear the mixed voice.

That's why the first time you hear your own voice tape recorded, it sounds thin and disappointing.

Are you disappointed?

No longer, but the first time I was crushed.

"That's not me."

Just so.

I find very interesting the way your body of work seems to be much like you speak. In your poem "Attention Shoppers" you write:

> There's a blue light special in Aisle Six.
> We've mounded toddlers' sneakers higher than desire.

KMart talk slides into verse and vice versa. And you write much like you talk and vice versa.

It does go both ways. Some American poets think of writing like they talk as a sign of achieved sincerity, and often William Carlos Williams is invoked as the patron saint of the vernacular. Williams is a more complex poet than such endorsements allow, and the trouble with the model is that it only moves one way, from speech to writing.

If you teach for a living, you're continually alert to how you speak to whom. You chide some, goad some, praise some, joke with others. This kind of talk is very purposive and rhetorical. By contrast, writing can be amblier and less aimed. A little of the one, it seems possible, is good for the other.

So there are certain discoveries that you make as you teach that you would never make as a student?

I suspect that the most interesting things you learn from teaching you're not aware of learning: they seep in while you're concentrating on something else.

But here's something I noticed in a Roethke seminar I've been teaching. Everyone in the class is a graduate student in creative writing. We'd talked about Roethke's essay "How to Write like Somebody Else" early in the semester and were reading the late long poems. I read some lines from "Meditations of an Old Woman," where Roethke sounds somewhat like Eliot, and some lines from "North American Sequence," in which he wrangles with Stevens in Stevens's characteristic diction and rhythms. We weren't talking about "influence" or "allusion" but about the literary equivalent of a familiar social phenomenon: that we vary our speech slightly but noticeably according to who's listening. Roethke had learned to address, even to invoke, certain parts of his poetic imagination by adopting the diction and rhythms of the poets he associated with those varied territories. I suddenly realized that he must have learned this from teaching, from the way a teacher shares a slightly different dialect with each person in a class.

Probably the students learned something quite different, but it's a dull class in which everyone learns the same thing.

Sounds like a good class.

I thought so. But then there's next week. . . .

In Raymond Carver's book A New Path to the Waterfall *Tess Gallagher tells in her introduction how Carver referred to someone's accusation that Tchaikovsky had lifted a passage from Beethoven. Tchaikovsky said, "I have a right. I love it." Carver told the story to illustrate his use of Chekhov. How do you feel about the influence of one poet on another or one art form on another?*

We're primates. We learn by imitation, which in this context means not flattery but gratitude. Young jazz musicians learn to play solos by the masters note for note, as a way of feeling what it would be like to think your way through a great solo. It sharpens your technique, of course, but also it gives you a sense of what can built on the tradition if you'll go to school there.

If you strive to be original, you can cut yourself off from your origins.

Let's talk a little now about the structures of poetry and music, about bones and muscles. In your poem "By Heart" you write

Which came first, style or content? To this trick
question Drs. Xtl and Yrf and Professor Zyzgg
have given honorable gray hours . . .

I haven't figured out how to say those names.
   You can't.
   How did I know that? It took hours.

      . . . have given honorable gray hours. Style is that rind

   of the soul that we can persuade to die with us—
   no wonder we call it a body of work. Suppose
   style is the man or woman, the crumbling reams

   of shale, the mango, the brine shrimp, the world
   as it is. Is content then what the world isn't?
   I don't think so. Content is what style's failed.

What's going on here?
   If content is what style's failed, then content is what's imma-
terial and unembodied, I suppose, and thus left out of the body
of work.
   The soul becomes what, then?
   If we could articulate everything, if we could, in effect, take it
with us, there'd be nothing "left over," as the teacher said when
she explained long division.
   But we can't. I don't know if what remains mute and ghostly
has the greater glory. We seem to elevate soul over body, but
then familiarity and contempt have small access to the soul.
   Silence is, of course, the direst enemy of poetry or music. I
don't mean "rests" or spaces. I mean what we didn't name or say
that we might have named or said. This accumulation has a
glum, terrifying power. We could call it "God," if by *God* we
mean that which we can't humanize. If this is the soul, it's a
failed body. We couldn't make it mortal, so it haunts us.
   And it's the poet's or musician's need to make things mortal?
   Yes. To make it dust so it can return to dust. Duff. Litter.
Rind. Too, too solid flesh.
   Perhaps what the spirit would really like to be, if we were
adept enough to transform it, is matter.

Poetry & Music

The power of music that poetry lacks is the ability to persuade without argument.

Orpheus could make the stones move and the trees shake. The closest claim in American poetry to such magic is the one Wallace Stevens made for his jar in Tennessee, and we all know that to anyone not a poet nor a gifted and passionate reader of poetry the landscape, after the jar has been placed in it, looks exactly the same, except there's a jar in it. It's by envy of his powers that poets are forced to admit it: Orpheus was a musician.

In order for us to be moved by a poem—and this is the interior equivalent of the stones shifting about—an assent is required. We concur, somehow, with the proposition of a poem. We let it confide in us. Some part of this curious transaction, not the major but a crucial part, requires an intellectual assent. It's the rest of the transaction that invites comparisons between poetry and music.

Music happens to us in "real time." Indeed, to change the time of a piece of music is to alter, as it were, its cellular makeup, and for the worse. But for those who really love a poem, stopping, musing, going back and rereading it, are forms that love takes. So that's not the similarity.

It may be easier to think about the source of the long habit of comparing poetry and music by comparing the way speech happens to us with the way we read a poem on the page.

Here, too, we can make a recognizable distinction: speech happens in real time, and poetry doesn't.

But there's a more important distinction.

If I'm speaking to you, I'm also moving my hands, changing facial expressions, leaning toward you or away or carefully main-

taining the same distance, etc. "Body language," this is collo-
quially called, and it's a considerable rhetorical arsenal.

When poetry happens to you on the page, all of this is miss-
ing, and it's what poets do to compensate, on the page, for the
loss of body language that invites us to comparisons between po-
etry and music. It's when we speak of the poet's skill that we
speak of "voice" and "tone" and "phrasing" and "rhythm," etc.

The precise meanings of such words are famously difficult to
pin down, and necessarily so, for the phenomena they describe
are elusive, real shape-shifters, and the vocabulary we use to
refer to them had better be elastic.

"Form" is what we call it when it's dormant, when the poem
is adoze on the page and no reader comes to wake it. But read
with it your eyes, speak it in your silent voice, experience it with
your body—the reader, too, has a body of work—and you'll find
it mutable, swift, varied in its particulars and yet all of a piece,
like music or running water.

Perhaps I was wrong to suggest that a reader's intellectual assent
to a poem is in some way a precondition to participating in
those behaviors of a poem that we like to liken to music. That's
certainly not the way jump-rope rhymes and lullabies work on
their audiences.

I would be similarly wrong to imply the reverse, that the "mu-
sical aspects" of a poem trigger the assent.

Neither causes the other. Rather, they're aspects of the same
event, that heightened attention and deepened perception that
we release in ourselves in the presence of a good poem.

The inherited vocabulary of prosody and literary criticism can
all too easily induce a taxonomic hypnosis in which both writer
and readers are all too confident that they know exactly what's
under discussion. But the urge to describe the effects of poetry
in musical vocabulary is resistant to exact description in discur-
sive English. Indeed, most of our emotional lives are resistant to
exact description in discursive English.

And that's why there are, now and then, essays (in the etymo-
logical sense of *essay*, from the Latin *exigere*, "to weigh"—think of
the English *assay*—and thus a trial, a try, an attempt) like this
one, which is a revery on the reason why there are, now and

then, essays like this and, now and then, a few readers for such reveries: once the schools had taught us to read and then to write discursive English, we hedged our bets and didn't discard the poetry that had brought us that far.

Butterscotch Ripple

The reason Dick Hugo came to Boulder, a boutique at the foot of the mountains and the spiritual-growth-without-pain hotspot of America, was to raise his salary at the University of Montana. They were paying him eighteen thousand dollars—a smugly small salary. Perhaps the poobahs in Missoula had the disease of the provinces: if it comes from here, it's not worth much. We would very much have liked him to come teach at the University of Colorado, but we knew all along Dick would parlay our offer into a small raise at Montana and go back, and so we treated his academic year (1974–75) with us as a gift.

That spring Dick and I drove to Ft. Collins to give a weekend workshop at Colorado State. There would be a mixture of CSU student writers and writers from the community. In the event they made a very pleasant group, with one great talent hidden among them—a young and not very talkative Yusef Komunyakaa.

We stocked Dick's mammoth Buick convertible with a batch of congenial tapes—Pee Wee Russell and Mozart. We set out, bantering like guys in a buddy movie, but about halfway (the trip takes an hour) Dick fell silent.

"What are you thinking of?" I asked him.

Dick wasn't drinking. "Vodka," he said. "I could sit on one of those porches," he said, lifting a vast shoulder in a Montana version of a Gallic shrug, "and drink vodka and stare moodily into space." The houses we passed were between towns and far apart; they shimmered with depressed solitude. We came to a town border, and a sign gave the town's name and altitude.

"Who cares how far up this burg is?" he cackled. "I want to know how many people live here, or (a pause worthy of Jack Benny) how few."

Dick missed the booze, of course, but it was something the

booze made possible, for which booze was the surest first step, that he missed even more: shame and shame's isolation.

Years after our trip to Ft. Collins, only a few weeks before he died, Dick drove from Missoula to Seattle, where I lived then, to catch all four games of a series between the Mariners and the Yankees. I know from his poems that he was beaten when a child. "It's our fault," I once heard a class-full of second-graders spout in unison, lined up by size-places on the sidewalk in front of a parochial school on the block where I now live in New York City. The teacher loomed over them like the statue of a great tax collector and made them say it twice.

Once we got in, Dick was happy. A motel room, a ball game on TV, no duties (and those only social) till dinner. We were mid-meal when the English department chairman came over to pay Dick his respects. "I've read every one of your novels," he said.

"Poems," Dick corrected him gleefully.

"Of course that's what I meant to say," the chairman stammered and left.

"Now *that*," Dick pronounced, "was a magnificent phony."

Next day we conducted a workshop. What made Dick a great teacher was not only what he knew about writing poems but also his sense that writing was emotionally crucial. "When you write you are momentarily telling the world and yourself that neither of you need any reason to be but the one you had all along," he wrote in *The Triggering Town.*

He knew that funny criticism was easier for a student to accept than pontifications. In fact, such criticism invites the student to laugh at his worst impulses, to separate himself from them with the grace and violence of humor. "I want to hold you forever" was a line in one poem we were given that day.

"Bill, what do you think about the line?" he asked me, and, while I paused to see what bromide about clichés I'd use that day, Dick turned to the writer.

"What if you need to pee?" he asked.

Later, back at the motel, we had a swimming pool to wallow in, a baseball game on TV in front of which Dick could do his imitation of a third base coach giving the hitter the triple sign (three fingers), and some ice cream Dick had bought on the way from the workshop. Dick had a game leg, and I'd offered to hop out of the car and do the shopping, but shopping for junk food, pale as it was compared to drinking vodka alone, offered a small parody of shameful isolation, so he gimped in and shopped.

Then, back at the motel, he asked if I wanted some ice cream. "Yes" was of course the right answer, but I had lots to learn. I was very consciously discriminating in those years.

"What kind is it?" I asked.

"It's not tasteful enough for you," he said. "You probably like really good vanilla."

I might have flinched. He had me pegged.

"I like it," he said, "when you take some glop and some ice cream and swirl it all together."

Old Haunts

A writer is neither born nor made but written. Thus one of the pleasures of reading these autobiographical essays by Richard Hugo is to watch one of our central poets recapitulate, late in his life and at the peak of his powers, the long process of building a life's work (q.v., *Making Certain It Goes On: The Collected Poems of Richard Hugo* [1984]). But, in writing the essays, the poet has the accumulated momentum and insight of the poetry. He knows how the story comes out, and thus at relevant points in the narrative he can quote aptly from his own work. *Yes,* he seems to be saying in pleased recognition, *that's the man I became.*

So this remarkable book is neither a conventional autobiography nor that rarer thing, the autobiography of a body of work, but, rarest of all, an extended meditation on the relationship between the life and the work.

The life, after all, could be given in brief synopsis. Dave Smith has a wonderfully acute and empathetic paragraph in his essay "The Man from White Center."

> Fatherless and abandoned by his teenage mother, Hugo was raised by elderly, severe grandparents in White Center, Washington, then a semi-rural, poor suburb of Seattle. Enforced churchgoing left him feeling he owed something, spiritually dunned all his life. Shy, awkward and isolated, he believed himself not only the cause of his ill fortunes but also unregenerately weak, worthless, and ever "a wrong thing in a right world." He grew up admiring local toughs for their violent courage. He extended this admiration later to sardonic movie stars, detective heroes, and British Royal Air Force flyers, who

First appeared as the introduction to Richard Hugo's posthumous *The Real West Marginal Way: A Poet's Autobiography* (New York: W. W. Norton, 1986).

44

seemed to have a stylish, right manhood. He feared, hated and coveted girls and compensated by making himself a skilled baseball player, fisherman, and dreamer. His tutelary spirits appeared early and never abandoned him—waters, sky, hills, ocean, fish, birds and drunks. All meant unimpeachable and continuous acceptance, private dignity, and sweet, if un-recognized, belonging.

The tutelary spirits pervade these essays. "The Anxious Fields of Play" is perhaps the most unsentimental hymn to baseball in English, and Hugo's love of waters, fishing, and friendship is everywhere in this book. I remember Hugo settling contentedly before a television set in anticipation of an afternoon of base-ball. "As you know," he pronounced, "work is ridiculous."

Hugo had the loner's natural gift for friendship, and he watched baseball, drank, fished, and made excursions with a re-markable number of people. His outings were famous, and the fifteen poems called "Montana with Friends" and eleven poems called "Touring with Friends" from *The Lady in Kicking Horse Re-servoir*, each poem dedicated to somebody who shared the trig-gering event, are testimony to how gregarious Hugo taught him-self to be.

"Ghost in a Field of Mint," dedicated to Sister Madeleine De-Frees (DeFrees was then a nun), is a good example of the genre.

> The old man on the prison work release gang
> hoeing asphalt followed us to Wilkeson
> and those cyrillic graves, to Carbanado
> and that one long empty street, Voight's Creek
> and then Kapowsin and our picnic
> in a field of mint. Wherever we went, old haunts
> I wanted you to see, he hung there grim.
> I ruined him with theory: sodomy, infanticide.
> His bitter face kept saying we die broken.
> Our crab pate seemed bitter and the sun.
>
> In old poems I put evil things in Carbanado
> where I'd never been because a word that soft
> and lovely must be wrong, must hide what
> really happened, the unreported murder
> in the tavern, faithless wives. Clouds were birds
> of prey. The cell door clangs before we know

we're doing wrong. The stern click of the calendar
damned us long ago to take pain on the tongue.

One day, alone in the asylum, I will find
a door left open and the open field beyond,
a wife beside that road the map forgot
waiting as prearranged.
She'll say, I'm crazy, too. I understand.
From then on we will seek the harboring towns,
towns you never find, those floweres dying
certain the forlorn die wise. My sister,
we have been released from the entire day.

The old man is a characteristic figure in Hugo's poems—
someone fallen irremediably into solitude, exile, and wretched-
ness, an emblem of self-pity. Each picnic or excursion is a cere-
mony against his baleful possibility. If pain is our daily bread,
then here's how we live with it.

It's interesting to note the poem's prediction of Hugo's later
happy marriage. But it's not a wistful hope or an uncanny fore-
shadowing. The ceremonies of friendship and outings were a
preparation for happiness, and it was not *for* but *by* such good
behavior that a reprieve longer than a day was achieved.

The essay on James Wright is a moving portrait of Wright's
and Hugo's rhyming temperaments and another glimpse of
Hugo's practicing affection. The last years of his life he came
frequently to Seattle, and in those days I was living there. Some-
times we'd go to the Kingdome and watch through conditioned
air baseball being played indoors, an event even more ridicu-
lous than work. Sometimes we'd just drive around. There were
old haunts he wanted me to see—White Center, the Pike Place
Market, a place where a houseboat he'd lived on long ago had
been moored. I was glad for the looks into his life, and for his
company, but I knew the jaunts were as much for him as for me.
He was always homing.

The last time he was in Seattle I'd go to the hospital to sit with
him and watch baseball on television. We watched through the
playoffs and then into the Series, but between the sixth and sev-
enth games his condition grew suddenly far worse, and then he
died swiftly. Baseball, its fans love to say, is the only team sport
not played with or against a clock. But no game is more about

mortality. Fouling them off, a batter is said to be staying alive. He only gets, according to conventional wisdom, one good pitch to hit per appearance at the plate. A team has only twenty-seven outs to spend. And in the box score the next day one of the statistics the game will have produced is how long it took to play the game. Hugo's life wasn't anywhere near long enough for the many who loved him.

But he died with many loving him, with a wonderful body of work, with the marriage and family he struggled so hard to feel worthy of. He was in many ways a single-minded man. His work shows a similar consistency. He found a unique and flexible style early, and rather than modify it he clarified and simplified it, making familiar and capable what at first might have seemed idiosyncratic.

A late poem, "Glen Uig," begins with a couple on an outing to the Faery Glen. Here's the last stanza.

> Believe the couple who have finished their picnic
> And make wet love in the grass, the wise tiny creatures
> Cheering them on. Believe in milestones, the day
> You left home forever and the cold open way
> A world wouldn't let you come in. Believe
> You and I are that couple. Believe you and I sing tiny
> And wise and could if we had to eat stone and go on.

These essays don't give us, then, a different autobiography from the poems, because their primary interest, after all, isn't autobiography per se but the relationship between a poet's life and work.

If the book took on the obligations of conventional autobiography, it would require reference to Hugo's first marriage, for example. The title poem of *What Thou Lovest Well Remains American* gives us these chilling lines.

> Lawns well trained remind you of the train
> Your wife took one day forever, some far empty town,
> The odd name you never forget. The time 6:23.
> The day October 9. The year remains a blur.

Hugo's poems tell us how much his happy marriage to Ripley Schemm kindled and warmed his last years and how thoroughly involved he rapidly grew with her children from a previous marriage. But, except for the sense of guilt for the failure of his first marriage that pervades all but his late poems, what do we know of his first wife? Little from the poems and less from the essays. At the memorial evening for Hugo the Academy of American Poets sponsored in the spring of 1984 at the Guggenheim, Carolyn Kizer spoke of Hugo as lucky to have been married to two wonderful women.

My argument here isn't that Hugo should have included an essay on his first marriage but that the absence of one tells us a great deal about how to understand the relationship between his life and work.

Surely Hugo felt loss and even abandonment, and surely he was fiercely and sometimes helplessly (the ferocity may well be in direct proportion to the helplessness) loyal to the circumstances of loss and abandonment. But this is a book about trying to get home. It is given, here as everywhere in Hugo's work, that we're all lost and abandoned.

Isn't our fascination with loss dangerous to us precisely because what we most grieve for is not what we honestly lost but what we never had and which therefore no amount of imaginative fervor can ever restore to us? It's too much to lug home.

"In a way, all towns you look at could be your home town," Hugo said in his *Ohio Review* interview.

We know the towns, or town, he meant. Some of its names are Kalalock, La Push, Gooseprairie, Mukilteo, Tahola, Bear Paw, Philipsburg, Nine Mile, and Ten Sleep. There are Italian names (Tretitoli, Maratea, Acqufredda) and Scottish names (Uig, Ayr). There are more specific locations: West Marginal Way, 1614 Boren, the Milltown Union Bar, and Spurgin Road field. Some are names of places, poems, and whole states of mind, all at once:

> Helena, Where Homes Go Mad
> Where Jennie Used to Swim
> What the Brand New Freeway Won't Go Past
> Where Mission Creek Runs Hard for Joy

The meaning of the profusion is not just a rich life and a bottomless longing for connection, though Hugo had both. And the meaning isn't primarily that Hugo could find emblems of the collision between communal optimism and private degradation, between planning and loss, between courage and failure, wherever he turned his gaze.

The meaning of the profusion is that the process is endless. For to say "all towns you look at could be your home town" is not only to say you are homeless but that you are potentially at home anywhere. It is to say along with Whitman that you can, by continuous imaginative appropriation, belong to America, however beautifully and terrifyingly vast it is. And it is to say that the continuous reclamation of a hometown, the original mystifying poise between self and others, is the lifelong imaginative project of any adult.

There are specialized ways to carry out this work more formally and purposively than usual, and Hugo used two of them: psychotherapy and writing. Here and there in the poems we see residue from psychotherapy.

> You conquer loss
> By going to the place it happened
> And replaying it, saying the name
> Of the face in the open casket right.

The passage reminds us of those moments in Hitchcock's films (*Psycho, Marnie*) where the complexity of personality and psychic life is suddenly compromised by a need for explanation. And it seems to be the nature of self-regard that it is a process without a clearly definable product or explanation.

The passage about the open casket fits psychoanalytic theory neatly enough, and that's finally the problem. It has the relationship to the process that theology has to God. What's interesting about Hugo's urge to write the lines is the explicit parallel between whatever he learned from psychotherapy and his relentless homing, which is not explained by his poems or these essays but is beautifully embodied by them.

Seen in this light, all Hugo's work (including his book of pedagogical essays, *The Triggering Town,* and his mystery novel, *Death and the Good Life*) is the work of ceaseless reclamation.

Each town was a new opportunity. I remember driving with Hugo from Boulder to Fort Collins to conduct a workshop in 1976. When we got in we'd take motel rooms and then convene in Dick's to watch baseball and eat ice cream. Dick went in for flavors whose names ended in *brickle, twirl,* or *ripple.* He liked things stirred up and impure. At the workshop he would criticize a sentiment like "I want to hold you forever," not by describing it as a cliché but by asking "What will you do when you need to pee?' But this was ahead of us. We were driving along the Colorado foothills and Dick was reading out the names of the small towns we passed through. "Damn it!" he called out after a few miles. "Who cares what altitude they're at? Why don't these signs give the population?"

I think he wanted to know not how many but how few people lived in those towns. Always room for one more.

Layered Vision

Seen from afterward the time appears to have been
  all of a piece which is of course how it was but how
      seldom
it seemed that way when it was still happening and was
  the air through which I saw it as I went on thinking
of somewhere else in some other time whether gone
  or never to arrive and so it was divided
however long I was living in it and I was where
  it kept coming together and where it kept moving
      apart
while home was a knowledge that did not suit every
  occasion
  but remained familiar and foreign as the untitled days
and what I knew better than to expect followed me
  into the garden and I would stand with friends among
the summer oaks and be a city in a different
  age and the dread news arrived on the morning when
      the plum trees
opened into silent flower and I could not let go
  of what I longed to be gone from and it would be that
      way
without end I thought unfinished and divided
  by nature and then a voice would call from the field
in the evening or the fox would bark in the cold night
  and that instant with each of its stars just where it was
in its unreturning course would appear even then
  entire and itself the way it all looks from afterward
                                    (W. S. Merwin, "Completion")

From *Field*, no. 57 (fall 1997).

The passage of time has always been Merwin's central, goading subject. You can't see it—breath, spirit, ghost. Invisible itself, its effects are almost everything we see: the roiling leaves, the taxi's blue plume of exhaust, the scroll of clouds across the brightening and then the darkened sky. Like Merwin's 1992 prose book, *The Lost Upland,* his recent book of poems, *The Vixen* (1996), is set in southwestern France and driven by a kind of layered vision.

Do you remember the biology books in which there were transparent overlays—one depicted the skeleton, one the musculature, one the circulatory system, and so on? When the student peered down through all the layers, a whole human anatomy was visible. Everything seemed more jumbled together and confusing than the subway system under Columbus Circle, but something complete had been made knowable from its easier-to-look-at components.

In *The Vixen* we see time most readily by its fragments and seldom whole. These few lines from "Old Sound" provide another example:

> many lives had begun and ended inside there
> > and had passed over the stone doorsill and looked from
> > > the windows
> to see faces arriving under trees that are not
> > there any more with the sky white behind them and
> > > doorways
> had been sealed up inside the squared stones of their
> > frames.

The poems in *The Vixen* abound in temporal disjunctions like the one in which "faces arriving under trees that are not / there any more with the sky white behind them" both unites two distinct times and insists on their absolute separation. The poem ends, a few lines later, still thinking about the palimpsest of times the house is:

> now its age is made of almost no time a sound
> > that you have to get far away from before you can hear it.
> Here's the beginning of "Bodies of Water."
> In the long stone basin under the apple tree
> > at the end of one spring in the garden I saw the faces
> of all the masons who had built there on the edge

> of the rock overlooking the valley their reflections
>   smiled out from the still surface into the speechless
>   daylight each of them for the moment the only one

It takes a steady sentry to see these moments of completion, for, as one of the poems in *The Vixen* ends, "something keeps going on without looking back."

The book is full of memorable, summary last lines. Here's a bouquet of them.

Most of the stories have to do with vanishing.

ૐ

it went as it came and the fragile green survived it

ૐ

if any of this remains it will not be me

ૐ

each of them coming from what was already gone

The interiors of the poems in this book are frequently rehearsals of the ways we experience time in fragments and think by shifting from fragment to fragment. Consider the last three lines of "Completion":

> and that instant with each of its stars just where it was
>   in its unreturning course would appear even then
>   entire and itself the way it all looks from afterward

It was after translating Jean Follain's unpunctuated poems (that book appeared in 1969) that Merwin followed suit. The rich ambiguities of the three lines quoted here can perhaps best be savored by following the pronoun *it* on its shape-shifting way through all three lines. It appears five times: (1) possessive form, meaning "the instant's stars"; (2) the instant; (3) the instant has an unreturning course because time goes one way only, although the stars that instant contains make us think of orbits, or returning courses, even though stars are suns and have no courses but are still while their planets circle them; (4) the instant itself, again; (5) this last *it* now means something vast, like a vista from which the instant and its place in a larger scheme can all be seen.

To punctuate those three lines would be to reduce their ambiguity and wrongly to housebreak them.

In those three final lines "Completion" shows us in microcosm the extraordinary accomplishment of these poems: over and over they enlist us in partial experiences and understandings of time and then lead us from that choreographed disjunction to the austere clarities of the book's many aphoristic final lines.

A Note on Prose, Verse, and the Line

"Lack of a firm sense of the line is a handicap," writes John Haines in *Field,* no. 9 ("Further Reflections on Line and the Poetic Voice"), and asks, "Is this why the prose poem is so much in evidence these days? There you don't have to justify your lines, just make the paragraph and let it go."

Haines uses *justify* not in the typesetter's meaning but in its religious meaning; writers of prose poems are like the lilies of the field.

I imagine one is drawn to write prose poems not by sloth, more purely practiced in hammocks, but by an urge to participate in a different kind of psychic energy than verse usually embodies.

Here are excerpts from etymologies of *prose* and *verse* in *Webster's Third New International Dictionary. Prose* is "fr. L *prosa,* fem. Of *prosus* straightforward, direct." *Verse* is "fr. L. *versus* row, line, verse; a kin to L *vertere* to turn."

So the line in prose is like a fishing line, cast out as far as it will go, straightforward. And the line in verse goes out from the margin, turns back, goes out again, etc. Thus poetry is often linked to dance. The serpentine line of verse goes more down the page than across it.

I think of the long lines tending toward prose in Blake's prophetic books, Whitman, visionary passages from Ginsberg and Roethke. Such poems are questing, tentative, discursive—fr. L *discursus* (past part. of *discurrere,* to run about)—rather than direct. But in them the line takes on some of the characteristics we stereotypically associate with prose.

From *A Field Guide to Contemporary Poetry and Poetics,* edited by Friebert and Young (Oberlin, Ohio: Oberlin College Press, 1980).

Short-lined, rhyming, metrically regular poems would presumably accommodate a different kind of psychic energy.

But counterexamples abound. I don't intend to propose laws, rather to notice that such tendencies, familiar to poets from memories—conscious and unconscious—of reading poems, are among the many factors influencing their decisions about lines.

The Poetry Blues

"The truth is," Hayden Carruth writes in a concluding sentence to one of the essays in *Sitting In: Selected Writings on Jazz, Blues, and Related Topics* (1986), "whether for good or ill and to the extent—is it any at all?—that we enjoy freedom of choice in this world, poetry for me was, and is, second-best to jazz."

"To my mind Schopenhauer was right when he suggested that the other arts aspire to the condition of music," Carruth writes in another essay, "except that I wish he had said 'ought to aspire.'" And elsewhere he quotes Nietzsche: "Without music life would be a mistake."

In "Mystery and Expressiveness" Carruth describes a talk he has given several times. He plays a blues by Billie Holiday.

> At the end is a one-bar tag by [Ben] Webster on tenor, and at the very end, just after the final beat but while the tone is still sounding, somebody moans. It is scarcely audible, but in my talk I play the final bars again with the volume turned up so that the audience can hear it easily. . . . Then I ask the audience what this moan means.

The impossibility of an exact answer to this question is what makes music so hard to write about and, interestingly enough, is exactly what makes the enterprise so precious to Carruth.

"Got Those Forever Inadequate Blues," another essay is called, and in it Carruth writes that

> [I] can never arrive at a linguistic formulation of the musical expressiveness of the blues. The best I have been able to do so far is to say that it is a sensual experience of seeking and failing, that is, of inadequacy.

From the *Seneca Review*, no. 1 (1990).

The blues may be "the musical expression of existentialist thought and feeling," as Carruth goes on to say, but I doubt it. In this formulation the urge of prose argument to elicit agreement from a reader has replaced something direct and impervious to reason that is the source of music's power. Music can persuade without soliciting consent, and that's what Carruth, and any poet in his or her right mind, envies.

Carruth is one of those poets for whom the inexpressible and the unspeakable are the best ambitions of language, so that writing is necessarily an experience of seeking and failing. We're near a working definition of *desire,* if desire is understood to be a longing whose most likely capture is itself.

It's not that music is *about* desire; that moan can't be readily translated into language. It's that the love of music recapitulates desire. Carruth is not only a listener but has also been a player, and what musician—even, and perhaps especially even, the very finest—hasn't felt, in the gap between what he can hear in his head and what he can play on his instrument, a figure for human longing and imperfection? There are nights it feels like the figure for human longing and imperfection.

Jazz, blues, *and* related topics, the book's subtitle promises. There are twenty-five essays, interleaved by thirteen poems.

The best of the poems, "Freedom and Discipline," is Carruth's version of Dryden's "Ode on St. Cecelia's Day."

> Saint Harmony, many
> years I have stript
>
> naked in your service
> under the lash. Yes, . . .

Carruth begins with the combination of penitence and eroticism that is the central tone of this remarkable book. "Freedom and discipline concur / only in ecstasy," the poem finds a way to assert near its end, and the religious and sexual meanings of discipline and ecstasy are braided to identity.

Carruth includes literary essays on Tom McGrath and on *Middlemarch* that benefit wonderfully from their new context.

What kind of a novel is *Middlemarch,* he asks? Not a psychological novel, not a novel of manners, nor a philosophical novel.

"In fact not one principal is an interesting person." It is instead, Carruth decides, "a meditative lyric in prose that uses . . . contrived anecdote to explore the failure of mankind in relation to [marriage]." It doesn't fit received categories of expectation and response but compels a powerful reaction, so what is it? An embodiment of longing. A book about seeking and failing.

Carruth sees McGrath's work as misunderstood and underloved because it, too, falls outside our learned habits of reading. McGrath's body of work is sprawled and uneven, but the examples Carruth gives are commandingly beautiful.

Less well received by the context are a review of James Wright's *Collected Prose* and an appreciation of Robert Duncan, but they're interesting in themselves. Carruth could write as a learned critic if he wanted to, but his manner is more like Virginia Woolf's or Randall Jarrell's; he writes as a reader who happens to be a writer.

Except he has nearly a theory, actually a set of variations on an unstated and inexpressible theme—though *theme* is the wrong word for the moan that ends the Billie Holiday blues.

"I am not a musicologist, but a poet," Carruth says in a footnote, but his essays "The Blues Scale" and "Influences: The Formal Idea of Jazz" are theoretically sound; he knows his stuff.

But he prefers "technical criticism" (e.g., Gunther Schuller's *Early Jazz*) to "impressionistic writing, . . . the kind of thing done by Whitney Balliett, . . . [which] exploits the reader by promising what it cannot deliver, an explanation or at least a description of the expressiveness of jazz, which every fully engaged listener longs for."

Schuller's work is exacting but his prose turgid. Balliett can write with grace and a fidelity to his own listening experience that has nothing to do with the slur in "impressionistic," which implies that our sensory grasp of music is not the beginning of the urge to music criticism but somehow an impediment to it.

The problem is, as Carruth insists throughout, that what jazz expresses is otherwise inexpressible. That's why the collective invention of jazz is so important: it expands our range of access to our emotions. That we can't explain how this works in discursive prose reminds us how much we needed jazz and shouldn't be, for poets, a first instance of the limits of discursive prose.

As Carruth says, the blues scale cannot be objectively notated. "It is subjective. It is an understanding that is felt. Is this a monstrous obstacle? Not at all. The understanding can be transmitted by the simplest means, i.e., from ear to ear."

What kind of understanding is this?

In "The Guy Downstairs" Carruth describes sitting down with the pianist Don Ewell, in Ewell's flat, to play (clarinet is Carruth's instrument), and after the first few bars the guy downstairs would start to beat on the ceiling with a broom handle. "Sometimes he did it so quickly it seemed as if he must have been waiting there for us to begin." When it seems as if "the guy downstairs has taken over the world," when one feels an outsider, jazz and the blues can express it, and even better they contain the paradoxical knowledge that it is actually what seems most to isolate us from others, our shame, our solitude, our truculence, that is most human in us. And they give it voice.

Some of the understanding is about love. "The main thing, in jazz as in all the arts, is first to care, then to know, and finally to appreciate, i.e., to avoid and combat musicology and other such forms of pedantic historicism like the plague. To this main thing I have given a large part of my life, and I am glad of it."

Some of the understanding is about mixed feelings. Carruth is here, as in his poems, willing to be intellectually inconsistent, as in the case of technical criticism and musicology, because there's emotional truth in that ambivalence.

And there's real understanding available about race in American life. Performed or recorded jazz of course belongs to any listener who will meet it. But white people couldn't have invented jazz, and there was little in white American culture to suggest to us how badly we needed it. Carruth writes well on this topic, which has undone so many jazz writers. He's resistant to sweeping theories of all sorts, and this helps him. And of course he can hear in the music itself a kind of racial subplot, a "story," in the sense that early jazz musicians used the word to denote a solo that went somewhere rather than diddling in place. Part of that story is much of what most white Americans know about what it might be like to be black.

And part of that story is a visionary dream of "a great session where race has no ignificance at all . . . [and] every performer and listener participates freely and equally in the bodily and spiritually wrenching, exhilarating, purging experience of jazz-in-itself." It's with this dream that Carruth ends the last essay in his book.

"I dream the dream that I thought was an actuality when I was a boy. It cannot happen. But may we not go in that direction?" The best answer to that question is probably the moan at the end of the Billie Holiday blues.

Some Thoughts on
The Book of Nightmares

In his *Ohio Review* interview Galway Kinnell says, "That there are ten sections I suppose is in tribute to the *Duino Elegies*." His book begins with an epigraph from the fourth elegy.

> But this, though: death
> the whole of death,—even before life's begun,
> to hold it also gently, and be good:
> this is beyond description.

These lines suggest how spiritually ambitious and how self-consciously *big* Kinnell's poem is.

It's recurring words are like stones—*universe, emptiness, fear, darkness, flesh,* others of similar weight. And when large significances aren't directly invoked, they overlie the particular.

> A round-
> cheeked girlchild comes awake
> in her crib. The green
> swaddlings tear open,
> a filament or vestment
> tears, the blue
> flower opens.

Girlchild suggests the whole species, where *daughter* would specify. *Swaddlings* likewise link the girl to all children, as does *vestment.* The tearing filament, a generalized version of an umbilical cord, likens waking to birth. The enjambments in this

---

From *Stone Drum* (fall 1972).

passage underline its urge toward the large, the cosmic, the final. We get *the green, the blue,* just as the poem is not *A* but *The Book of Nightmares.*

The two main characters of this long poem are death and the narrator. The *Ohio Review* interviewer thinks that in *The Book of Nightmares* "there is a hero . . . , a character being created, and that he's going through certain experiences, and being confronted by certain tests, and that he will win or lose by the end of the story. Assuming he does lose, which he will in your poems, his life is being celebrated nevertheless." Kinnell concurs.

That character is certainly a representative figure, an Everyman, just as his daughter is a girlchild. He is facing death—not the philosophical problem of death, but death as a daily force, a trickster, a spiritual advisor, and perhaps the lover whose embrace we defer

> for reasons—cowardice
> loyalties, all which goes by the name "necessity"

until we discover that one of death's names is "necessity." The book is also, as its title suggests, a wisdom book. The *Ohio Review* interviewer speaks of it as "a book for children," by which I take him to mean a legacy. Kinnell speaks of the book as a "way of coping" and elsewhere in his interview mentions the desirability of poems "that could teach the way Rilke does, the way much of the best of Whitman does."

For all the courage and ambition, for all the weight of his own life, Kinnell has placed on his narrator and poem, I am grateful and heartened. But I am disturbed by a fatalism in his poem. Because I like the poem, and because I prefer poems that disturb rather than agree with or confirm me, I have read his poem again and again. And each time something has bothered me that I couldn't name until I read the *Ohio Review* interviewer speaking of Kinnell's main character: "Assuming he does lose, which he will in your poems. . . ." The poem is meant to be a tragic poem, so that its hero will "lose," according to the world's terms. But he will have won his own spiritual life. At the end of great tragedies the page and stage and mind are littered with corpses, eroded social order, failed ambitions, families turned against themselves, but we are strangely joyful because spiritual life has, even by all this damage, restored itself.

But at the end of *The Book of Nightmares* I feel a sense of false necessity. In his fourth poem Kinnell asks,

> Can it ever be true—
> All bodies, one body, one light
> Made of everyone's darkness together?

And in the tenth poem, as if in answer,

> On the river the world floats by holding one corpse.

What has happened in the meantime? The poem tells its own story, as all good poems do. My interest here is not to paraphrase it but to notice what in the poem makes its tragic dimension seem slightly mechanical to me. One way to notice that is to watch the themes of love and sexuality develop. The fourth poem ends:

> Never mind.
> The self is the least of it.
> Let our scars fall in love.

An important theme here is that love turns outward, away from the self, and so it can keep on going, past the lover, toward the universe. And yet it is the self that loves, even if it must love in spite of itself. And it is the lover's self that hopes to be not only one of the universe's multiple wonders but also a being that is itself before it is obscured by its cosmic role.

And so, just as the narrator's children are dramatis personae even before they are wholly emerged from the womb (see the fourth poem), women in the poem are emblematic figures, incomplete, because their grit and special textures are immediately dressed in vast significances. The narrator's wife, who appears in the poem for the first time when she is pregnant, is first seen sleeping:

> happy
> far away, in some other,
> newly opened room of the world.

These lines end the first section of the eighth poem. But in the second section the narrator paraphrases Aristophanes (who may have "made it all up, nightmared it all up / on the spur / of that moment which has stabbed us ever since"):

> that each of us
> is a torn half
> whose lost other we keep seeking across time
> until we die, or give up—
> or actually find her

"as I myself . . . actually found her." The narrator leaves this woman, this other half, for reasons—cowardice, loyalties, all that goes by the name *necessity*.

Back in bed with his wife ("she who lies halved / beside me," as opposed to she who lives halved anywhere else, so that geography—the element of choice is underplayed here as "cowardice"—replaces affection), the narrator thinks of an impersonal love, acted out by him on his wife.

> And the brain kept blossoming
> all through the body, until the bones themselves could think,
> and the genitals sent out wave after wave of holy desire
> until even the dead brain cells
> surged and fell in god-like, androgynous fantasies—
> and I understood
> the unicorn's phallus could have risen, after all,
> directly out of thought itself.

It seems that love and sexuality exist as ideas ("the brain kept blossoming" and "even the dead brain cells / surged and fell") in the universe, and we embody them. Desire is holy, but the gods are androgynous—this situation I find confusing. Am I in bed with this woman, I would ask myself, because androgynous gods have given me desire but no model for sharing it? And if she too isn't on a divine mission, will she take it personally? And suppose she sensed and was discomforted by, as I am, the imaginative links in Kinnell's poem between death and sex, perfection and sex? Even the dead brain cells surged and fell, as miraculously as the unicorn's phallus "could have risen" (not the less conditional *rose* or *rises*) "directly out of thought itself."

Later in the eighth poem the narrator wonders what would have happened if "I had stayed / with that woman of Waterloo."

> our faces
> inclined toward each other, as hens
> incline their faces
> when the heat flows from the warmed egg
> back into the whole being, and the sliver moon
> had stood still for us in the middle of heaven—
>
> I think I might have closed my eyes, and moved
> from then on like the born blind,
> their faces
> gone into heaven already.

Again, the poem conveys a sense of necessity—the hen's instinct, the egglike moon poised in an omen's position, the blind condemned at birth to sainthood. And again, at the same time, I respond to the poem's emotional intensity, to its consistent projection of its narrator's character, to the confluence and compression of its themes and images—I find myself saying, No. This is beautiful and mostly true. But it has become as true as it is, as consistent with itself as it is, by omission. It has omitted the real element of human choice, without which tragedy always seems stage-managed.

In *Field,* no. 7, Adrienne Rich's essay "Poetry, Personality and Wholeness: A Response to Galway Kinnell" answers an interesting essay by Kinnell, "Poetry, Personality and Death," in *Field,* no. 4. Both essays are important, and I recommend them. Near the end of her essay Rich writes, "I have thought that the sense of doom and resignation to loneliness endemic in such masculine poetry has to do with a sense of *huis clos,* of having come to the end of a certain kind of perception."

I've felt both much accused and much warmed by *The Book of Nightmares* and in a different way (because essays don't have, finally, the fullness that Kinnell's poems or, for that matter, Adrienne Rich's poem have) by her essay.

I lazily want her to tell me more about "a certain kind of perception." I know that I have written and read of doom and loneliness and seen them as inevitable in ways that my reactions to *The Book of Nightmares* and to her essay belie.

But if that perception is behind and in *The Book of Nightmares,* I know some things about it, partly because Kinnell writes so well—better than anyone else—about it and partly because I have shared that perception, even in ways I didn't know until I read and reread Kinnell's poem.

I know that I have sometimes used my children, and their mother, as imaginative props, as locations in an idealized landscape. Sometimes I have seen a woman as a half of something, or I have failed to chide her for seeing herself as a half of something. These accusations could be directed at almost any man. But I am also a man who writes and reads poems as if they were crucial, because I believe they are. And it occurs to me, reading *The Book of Nightmares* again, that a man's relationship to other people (and thus, by implication, to animals, plants, the landscape) is, if that man is willful and selfish, analogous to a male poet's worst possible relationship to his material. It can be a reflection of him, his imaginative failures can become moral laws, he can be pope of this religion, he can use the large word *Fate* to describe something very particular—his own perversity.

No recent book of poems poses this problem to me more clearly, more courageously, or more fully than *The Book of Nightmares.* Implicit in my earlier comments about a slightly mechanical tragedy operating in Kinnell's poem is a judgment that the poem raises certain issues it doesn't resolve. I first noticed these while thinking about the role the narrator's wife and children and the woman of Waterloo play in the poem.

Then I began to think how one of the poem's basic themes is the question of how much the imagination trusts itself. Does the imagination colonize reality, to put the question in baldly "po-litical" terms, or does it finally rejoin, by remaking, the reality from which it has been separated by its own energies?

> Somewhere
> in the legends of blood sacrifice
> the fatted calf
> takes the bonfire into his arms, and *he*
> burns *it*.

Though the poem does not bring this question to its skin, it is in the marrow of the poem. Kinnell keeps pushing the poem to-ward the universe, toward death, as if there were an answer there. When he does, his poem is, by the standards of an aes-thetic critic, "overwritten"; and there are places where the poem seems to me by almost any standards overwritten, pushed too hard toward the largest significances, as if the world and death were, finally, not enough. But this is what I love most about Kin-nell's poem. There are books that obsessively raise issues they can neither resolve nor ignore. In its ambivalence toward the imagination that has made it, it resembles such diverse American works as *Leaves of Grass, The Sound and the Fury, Pierre, The Sacred Fount,* the end of *Huckleberry Finn* (especially! If we imagine death to be the territory, what can be more Kinnellian than "lighting out for the territory"?), *On the Road, Lolita.*

With Adrienne Rich I believe that Kinnell, because his imagina-tion (like his rhetoric) is ambitious and deliberately excessive, has brought a certain kind of perception to a *huis clos,* a place with no exit. In doing this, he has, as he hoped, written a "teach-ing poem," not a poem that lectures. I think not only about what it means to be the specific male I am but also about what it means to trust and mistrust my imagination. I think about my life.

NOTES

Kinnell's poem is in ten parts; the Sothic calendar, one strand in Kinnell's rug of arcana and occult imagery, is divided into ten months.

The Kinnell interview is in the *Ohio Review* (fall 1972). During the interview Kinnell and his interviewer talk about the exalting effect of tragedy.

I rely on Walter Slatoff's *With Respect for Readers*, and especially on its fifth chapter, "The Discomforts of Reading," for some of my ideas about imaginations trusting and mistrusting themselves. Slatoff quotes Robert M. Adams, *Strains of Discord*, on "open form"; a "literary form . . . which includes a major unresolved conflict with the intent of displaying its unresolvedness." My ellipsis omits the most pedantic part of Adam's description; most of it needs translation. But it is interesting to compare his idea—his book appeared in 1958—of open form with that of Berg and Mezey (editors of *Naked Poetry*), who equate *open form* with *free verse*. Adams is trying to talk about spirituality; Berg and Mezey try to talk about meter.

Merida, 1969

for Russell Banks

We sat in the courtyard
like landlords and dispatched
teak-colored Manolo
at intervals for Carta Blanca,
and propped idiomatically
little wedges of lime on top
of the bottles like party hats.
O tristes tropiques. Our pretty
wives were sad and so were we.
So this is how one lives when he
is sad, we almost said out loud.
Manolo, we cried, and his tough
feet came skittering across
the blue, rain-streaked tiles.

Travel turned out to be no
anodyne, for we went home.
It was a sort of metaphor,
we now agree, a training
in loss. For if we'd been happy
then, as now we often are,
we'd have sat there in Merida
with its skyline of churchspires
and windmills, the latter
looking like big tin dande-
lions from which the fluff
had just been blown by wind
they couldn't hold, and we'd cry
Manolo, and beer would arrive.

Merida, 1969

I was first stirred to write "Merida, 1969" by looking at a watercolor of Merida used as the cover illustration for Elizabeth Bishop's *The Collected Poems, 1927–1979*. Miss Bishop herself did the drawing. I had been in Merida some fifteen years ago; an old friend, Russell Banks, and I had spent a week there with our wives, now our ex-wives. And Banks was about to arrive in Maine, where I wrote the poem, for a visit, and so I had been thinking about friendship, its duration, the mutual stories friends invent and revise. And, since Banks had recently remarried and I would soon remarry, I was prickly, sentimental, skeptical, alert. In short I was about to start work on a poem, and had a welter of musings, memories, notions, confusions, etc., to work with.

Miss Bishop's drawing is dated (1942), and perhaps that's why my title includes a date, though I may in any case have wanted to set the time and place quickly in the title. Probably there were in draft some lines that I had to write and reject before I found my first line; I no longer have any version of the poem but the one given here.

One thing I know about the form the poem took is that I didn't decide on it before I started work, as I sometimes do, nor did I assume the poem would find a form on behalf of its own urgencies, as I sometimes do. What I must have wanted was for the poem to hint at some possibilities from which I could choose some constraints, but not until I was a little way into the poem and could sense what manner of resistance (4 ohms? 8 ohms?) might serve it best.

From *Ecstatic Occasions, Expedient Forms: 85 Leading Contemporary Poets Select and Comment on Their Poems,* edited by David Lehman (Ann Arbor: University of Michigan Press, 1996).

What I wound up with was a sort of mirrored diptych, two fourteen-line stanzas, one recounting 1969 and one about knowledge in the present, one narrative and one reflective, each one using some of the same incidents and atmosphere. There would be an implied contrast, naturally enough. How much has changed in the interval? How much have we learned? If we knew then what we know now . . . ?

Of course the preceding paragraph is written with hindsight, rather than with the attentive bumbling and diligent indolence that accompany composition. What I remember about writing the poem is that somewhere about five or six lines along I sensed, the way people suddenly know what it is they would like to eat for lunch, that I'd like the stanza to be fourteen lines, that in the blank space between the two stanzas—yes, there should be two stanzas—there would be an invisible hinge, and that the poem could propose by such a form an implied relationship between the past and the present that the poem could question and doubt.

Probably Frost's "The Road Not Taken" is a sort of model for my poem, though on a sufficiently unconscious level that I had no thought of it nor of Frost while I was writing. We all remember the ending of that poem:

> I shall be telling this with a sigh
> Somewhere ages and ages hence:
> Two roads diverged in a wood, and I—
> I took the one less traveled by,
> And that has made all the difference.

We sometimes forget how differently the poem's speaker describes the two roads at the time he actually chose one of them.

>   long I stood
> And looked down one as far as I could
> To where it bent in the undergrowth;
>
> Then took the other, as just as fair,
> And having perhaps the better claim,
> Because it was grassy and wanted wear;
> Though as for that the passing there
> Had worn them really about the same,

And both that morning equally lay
In leaves no step had trodden black.
Oh, I kept the first for another day!
Yet knowing how the way leads on to way,
I doubted if I should ever come back.

The roads beckoned about the same, but later, when the plea-
sure of telling the story was part of the story's truth, and there
was much intervening life to explain, we could hear the poem's
speaker veer off again, this time away from incident and toward
shapeliness.

Two roads diverged in a wood, and I—
I took the one less traveled by,
And that has made all the difference.

"And I," he says, pausing for dramatic effect and then giving his
little anecdote a neat and summary dramatic effect that's in the
story but not in the original event. Though of course by this
stage in the life of the story each exists somewhat for the sake of
the other.

My friend, an able writer of stories, was coming to visit, and
one of the things I was mulling over was how stories work.

Fourteen lines was no accident. I've written a number of pale
sonnets, unrhymed and in a trimeter or tetrameter line that hov-
ers somewhat between so-called free verse and metrically regular
verse. It's a territory I've been attracted to by noticing how the
two modes, so often poised against each other in neat and false
opposition, want to be each other. Be that as it may, I've had
happy experience with fourteen-line poems, and so poising two
stanzas that length against each other, in ways I had yet to work
out, satisfied both my need for familiarity and my need for sur-
prise. With luck, then, the poem had a form to become, and I
had both the comforts and challenges of an apt form. . . .

How well this all turned out the reader may judge. The two
friends in my poem seem to behave about the same under ei-
ther disposition—the narrative past, in the first stanza, or the
past as understood along all the intervening time, in the sec-
ond. In this second and hypothetical life, they may or may not
be wiser, but they are happier, and manifest their happiness, as

they did in 1969, by sending for beer. And why not? How often do we get a chance to vacation like this? Won't it all seem like a dream in, say, fifteen years?

The equality of the two behaviors is at least made easier—and perhaps made possible, for all I know now, long after I wrote the poem—by the discovery of the form.

What else should I say about the form? Content is often un-settling or painful in poems, but form is play, a residue of the fun the poet had while working. Of course, like form and con-tent, pain and fun want to be each other. . . .

Awkward

The only word in English with *awk* in sequence.

Or, "awk," as English teachers—I'm one—write on student papers, meaning something between "This is unconventional" and "The nature of our language, as I understand it, resists this construction." Auk, it should be extinct.

Clumsy thinking: can one sprain a tongue? From a student paper: "Ahab was killed at the hands of Moby Dick." And from another: "There is no movement in the bowels of the earth."

Or, as Steve Dunn found (or was given) this one: "Things have got so bad they're committing celibacy in the streets." And, as Steve was swift to see, they are.

What are the important differences between social and private definitions of *awkward*?

If language should communicate, *awkward* means to increase the space between the speaker and the listener, already immense. (Porchia, in Merwin's translation: "I know what I have given you. I do not know what you have received." And is Porchia's first sentence true?)

If language is designed in part to cloud, as so much of it does—political speeches, insurance policy prose, bad poems, seduction rhetoric—which lapses in communication are *awkward* and which exact?

If language should embody what we feel, how can it be wrong, unless our feelings, as we know they often are, are tawdry and inadequate to what we experience? By experience, then, I must mean not only what we feel but also what we think we think about what we feel, so far as we can recover that feeling from what we think about it.

Awkward means without grace.

From *Unmuzzled Ox*, 4, no. 4.

Grace means you endure paradox gracefully, even if it arises from the language you live by.

Or language may live by you. It may be our most elaborate parasite. A swarm of habits urgent to please by repeating its successes and urgent to grow by sticking its historical tongue out. Blaah.

In a good guest too much civility can be awkward. Does it therefore follow that in a good host too awkward can be civil? "I'm human, too." How hard to say such a sentence without false and easily accurate pride.

Blunder along. To thine own self be true: as if you had a choice. And everywhere along the line, you do; you do.

Bad Lines

An interesting question is why poets who are more or less competent technically write bad lines. In an earlier essay, "Dishonesty and Bad Manners" (*New England Review* 3, no. 4), like this essay derived from a talk I gave at the Aspen Writers' Conference in 1977, I considered the poet's urge to appear wiser than he really is at the time he writes bad lines. *Appear* implies an audience and so a social context; thus bad manners—which I'll define briefly here as a wrong balance between the needs of the self and the needs of others—are germane. "Than he really is" refers to a transaction with the self and thus to honesty. I concluded the essay by describing the poet's great freedom and fearful responsibility—that he may well be inventing the story of his life and then may well be condemned to live it out. How crucial it is, then, to write as well as we can.

So in that essay I described, concentrating on the problems of the younger poet, the need to find an abiding imaginative relationship between the self and all that is outside it (but to which the self somehow and crucially belongs).

In this essay I want to explore the medium in which that imaginative relationship is struck. The generic name for that medium is time, of course, and the specific name, for purposes of this essay, is history. Two aspects of it I want to examine here are, first, the models for apprenticeship and authority that a young poet inherits and, second, the modern tradition of the avant-garde that a young poet inherits.

"Make it new," Pound implored. The curt phrase has become a slogan for us and a truism. For centuries translators have understood that the idiom of verse evolves steadily in English and

---

This essay first appeared in a slightly different form in *Shenandoah* 23, no. 3 (1982).

hence that the classics need to be translated again at regular intervals, lest even in translation they grow dated and slip into a past from which they can only be retrieved by specialists. This implicit recognition that a language itself and its poetry are organisms did not usually contain an injunction that poets actively promote the organism's growth; rather, it was assumed that, being an organism, it would grow.

But Pound, as we know, argued from different premises. One who sets out to fulfill Pound's instruction must have an ear finely tuned enough to hear an established style growling stiffly toward self-parody, a sense of literary history and poetic convention acute enough to distinguish surely between resonance and helpless mimickry, and sufficient technical skill and force of personality to add to the poetry of one's own age a recognizably new tone.

This is a job description daunting enough to discourage applicants. And where might they have learned the skills the job requires? In university literature classes? Creative writing classes? In a weekly workshop organized by writers who eschew or despise universities? At a summer writers' conference?

In eighteenth-century England, let's say, we could reach agreement among interested folk as to what constituted a literary education—some Latin; less Greek; maybe one modern language, probably French; fairly sure knowledge of the King James Bible; classical mythology, with Ovid as central text; and the canon of great English poetry.

Now in America we don't agree what a literary education is; have almost no institutions capable to administer even a bare outline of one in four years; have a canon of American poetry the components of which we argue about endlessly; and have very mixed American feelings about history, itself, which Henry James thought we suffered from a lack of and Henry Ford thought bunk.

The impossibility of providing an aspirant poet with the skills that Pound's challenge requires has produced a typical American mythological figure—a literary Paul Bunyan on the one hand, a literary self-made man on the other.

Whitman is the first of our poets in this mold, "Walt Whitman, an American, one of the roughs, a kosmos;" in a "Sun-Down

Paper" he wrote, "Who should be a better judge of a man's talents than the man himself?"

Pound saw how well the mold fit him. "Ignorant men of genius are constantly rediscovering 'laws' of art which the academics had mislaid or hidden," he said early in *ABC of Reading*.

Whitman and Pound invented, in addition to their own poetry, a new mythological figure for the American poet. The genius of their invention is that it addressed the question of where, given the reluctance and inability of American literary culture to establish a uniform literary education, poets might look for the authority of their apprenticeships, the source of their high standards and high ambitions. A further instance of their genius in this regard is how long before these questions were generally seen to be problematical Whitman and Pound framed their shares of the answering myth.

The poet they invented was largely self-educated; skeptical if not contemptuous of official learning and official history; and able by force of personality and intense sympathy to discover or imagine, and to express, alternate sources of authority.

Our prominent current versions of this mythological figure are often, by virtue of the alternate authority they claim, gifted, powerful, and idiosyncratic didacts. And often they are invested by early apprenticeship, by ambition, and by their disciples, with a lineage, a sort of apostolic succession, such as the one by which Charles Olson and Robert Duncan inherit some of their powers from Ezra Pound.

In other relevant cases—those of Wendell Berry, Robert Bly, Allen Ginsberg, and Gary Snyder—part of the poet's claimed authority is an achieved relationship to a body of historical practice or understanding.

For Berry the disciplines are agriculture, husbandry, and a sort of Jeffersonian punditry. For Bly there is a palimpsest of authorities: Jacob Boehme, Tibetan Buddhism, Sufism. . . . For Ginsberg various strains of Buddhist thought and practice combine with an urge to social prophecy and active philanthropy. And in Snyder Zen Buddhism and an old-time Protestant working-class theology of manual labor combine with his anthropological training to form his loosely defined sense of tribal poetry.

Poets like these—poets who are also teachers, even preachers—are working out of the same crisis that Whitman and Pound felt, that a literary education needs more or less to be invented by the young poet and, furthermore, that there isn't even a very robust Establishment to fulminate against and to test oneself by opposition to. When Pound speaks of "'laws' of art which the academics had mislaid or hidden," he is invoking a very American Bogeyman, the elite priest class that conceals from the common man a technology he needs to advance himself. But the invention won't work, as any of us knows who has ever watched a committee of academics bend down, like a rhinoceros, to spear a cheese rind on its horn.

But the situation is by now radically different than it was for Whitman or Pound. In their different ways Whitman and Pound asserted that the experience of the practitioner accumulated a kind of authority; this is an honorable and recognizable form of the work ethic and a way of tweaking the noses of theoreticians and taste purveyors. Poets would be the acknowledged legislators of poetry, and they would appeal for that authority to their own work and to either, in Whitman's case, the common experience of democratic man or, in Pound's case, the taste and learning of one who had bothered to invent rather than merely to inherit his literary education.

These strategies did not answer the question, except for Whitman and Pound, of where a literary authority might come from. But such strategies did make the question possibly moot.

Later generations using Whitman and Pound as models and responding, as every generation must, to the same problem, have behaved very differently. For one thing, such a mythological figure now has a tradition; what Whitman and Pound had to invent we inherit. And, for another, the sources of authority are often found rather than invented. Alternative theories of history and consciousness are offered as the real authority, the suppressed antidote to the manifest ills of official history and official culture.

At just this point the etymological slosh between *cult* and *culture* becomes instructive. *Cult* comes from the Latin *cultus* (worship); *culture* comes from French by way of Latin *cultura* (the *OED* gives the following interesting gloss: "cultivation, tending, in Christian authors, worship, f. ppl. Stem of colere: see CULT."). I recently had a very satisfying two-hour talk about Charles Olson with a Bay Area poet, who it turned out, had never heard of Elizabeth Bishop. This is not education, which includes curiosity; it is, with its clinging to inerrant texts, fundamentalism.

In another important way the religious diction implicit in *cult* is unavoidable. Notice how for Whitman and Pound the source of authority is the self and its product poetry. "This is what is meant by having authority, or being an author," runs the last sentence of Louis Simpson's *Three on the Tower.*

But the abnegation of the self is important to almost all the current inheritors of the Whitman and Pound model, though with the paradox implied by charismatic fundamentalists that they are powerful cult figures who proclaim the fragility of the self.

In Berry and Snyder the land is an inerrant text; in Bly and Ginsberg bodies of doctrine and practice confer authority, which is not made by the poems but infuses them. Snyder's title *The Real Work* is instructive; he means not the work of writing poems but the work of achieving a correct relationship to reality. Authority invests the work of writing and lives outside the work of writing.

Two serious problems for the young poet arise from such a view. One is that it implies that better poems can be written by, essentially, correct religious experience. It is as if we came to America, those of us whose ancestors were not already here, not to escape religious persecution but to invent our own forms of it. The second is that it invites a young poet to ignore that what has `believe ?` made, say, Gary Snyder so valuable a figure in our literary life will make others valuable, as if Snyder's peculiar and forceful needs were in no way individual, as if he were the product of an intellectual and spiritual technology that can work for you, too.

Increasingly, Matthew Arnold's middlebrow prediction that art would replace religion has come to seem a curse. I think this a particularly distracting prophecy to young writers, for it implies nothing about what a literary education or apprenticeship might be but implies, instead, that one needs only to find the road and tread it, another pilgrim.

Surely, then, one reason a young poet might write bad lines is from aspiration to an authority outside the poem at hand, from aspiration to join a club (the saved) by imitating its members.

Another way young poets line themselves up in relation to what they can understand literary history to be is to join the avant-garde.

> The fighting poets.
> The literary vanguard.
> The use of military metaphor reveals minds not militant
> but formed for discipline, that is, for compliance; minds
> born servile, Belgian minds, which can only think collectively.

So wrote Baudelaire, I don't know what he held against Belgians, but it's clear what they're a figure for. He means that if we pose the wisdom of our own thin sliver of time against the clichés of the past, we neglect how our wisdoms are unrecognized clichés. The myth of the revolution, the corrective repudiation of the past, the cleansing apocalypse (the ugliest form of this myth), is also finally religious: every age likes to be premillennial, the last age before the great conversion, the only age in which we can have both sin and reformation, and in that order. Art becomes a kind of deathbed conversion.

To think of a literary life at its beginning in terms of literary history is a mistake. It is one thing to produce work so original and valuable that it becomes, by its own authority, avant-garde, as Marianne Moore's resolute fidelity to her own strangeness led her to do. It would be another thing deliberately to join the avant-garde as if it were a club.

I think it equally unproductive for a young poet to set up shop against the avant-garde, as if to link arms with the poet's parent generation against the rude other children.

It is because it is easy to confuse the preceding generation of poets with one's own parents that such alignments seem attractive to young poets. They are usually establishing themselves as young adults at the same time they are trying to learn how to write better, and it would be economical if the same psychic work would benefit both endeavors.

But the endeavors are crucially different. Becoming an adult usually means leaving home and beginning to make a home for yourself; however much that home may come with time to resemble the home you have left. If your relationship with your parents has been stormy, this fact seems especially vivid. Even if your relationship with your parents was Edenic, adult life seems at first to be irretrievably not-home; happy childhoods are the hardest to grow away from, I suspect.

2 No

Literary tradition functions very differently. It is not inevitable that a young human becomes by continuous hard work a competent writer, whereas it is inevitable that a young human ages and nearly inevitable that leaving home is part of that process (though Marianne Moore lived always with her mother).

Literary tradition is a continuous transmission of skills, and though each generation operates by different aesthetic assumptions, and often finds it convenient to define those assumptions in contradiction to the assumptions of those older poets they have learned from, the continuity is more important and powerful than the disruptions. If the lines of transmission were ever wholly cut, we would be forced to teach ourselves entirely from books. Imagine the cuisine of a civilization in which no cook ever discussed the art with young cooks, and everything the young cooks wanted to learn had to be got from books written by elders for whom reticence was a virtue.

But many young poets assume that tradition, like parents, must be rebelled against. Since aging is inevitable and learning to write well isn't, and since growing older and learning to write well are different enterprises, young poets could save themselves wasted time by not imagining these two projects as identical or parallel.

Worries about lines of influence, lineage, lines marking the borders between official and unofficial knowledge, linking arms to form lines—all these worries seem likely to help young poets write bad lines from inattention to the main tasks: reading with a wide and heterodox curiosity, writing, and inventing from the many and informally organized sources available a literary present from themselves. Literary history will no doubt continue to take care of itself.

100 Sentences

Not that the story need be long, but it will take a long
while to make it short.
   —Henry David Thoreau

We will now discuss in a little more detail the struggle for
existence.
   —Charles Darwin

Grub first, then ethics.
   —Bertolt Brecht

Hope is a good breakfast, but it is a bad supper.
   —Francis Bacon

When he awoke, the dinosaur was still there.
   —Italo Calvino (example of a story
   complete in one sentence)

It was a terrible day and it hadn't even begun yet.
   —Len Deighton

Yet you ask on what account I write so many love-lyrics
And whence this soft book came into my mouth.
   —Ezra Pound

Appetite grows by eating.
   —François Rabelais

From the *New England Review* 14, no. 2 (spring 1992).

Come, woo me, woo me, for now I am in a holiday humor,
and like enough to consent.
   —Shakespeare

Nine-tenths of what we attribute to sexuality is the work
of our magnificent ability to imagine, which is no longer
an instinct, but exactly the opposite: a creation.
   —Ortega y Gasset

What fortitude the soul contains,
That it can so endure
The accent of a falling foot—
The opening of a Door.
   —Emily Dickinson

      Her pure and eloquent blood
Spoke in her cheeks, and so distinctly wrought,
That one might almost say, her body thought.
   —John Donne

We have left undone those things which we ought to
have done; And we have done those things which we
ought not to have done; And there is no health in us.
   —The Book of Common Prayer

One's real life is often the life that one does not lead.
   —Oscar Wilde

We think caged birds sing, when indeed they cry.
   —John Webster

They have a king and officers of sorts;
Where some, like magistrates, correct at home,
Others, like merchants, venture trade abroad,
Others, like soldiers, armed in their stings,
Make boot upon the summer's velvet buds;
Which pillage they with merry march bring home
To the tent-royal of their emperor:
Who, busied in his majesty, surveys
The singing masons building roofs of gold,

The civil citizens kneading up the honey,
The poor mechanic porters crowding in
Their heavy burdens at the narrow gate,
The sad-eyed justice, with his surly hum,
Delivering o'er to to executors pale
The lazy yawning drone.
  —Shakespeare

Great God! This is an awful place.
  —Capt. R. F. Scott, of the South Pole

Live with yourself: learn how poorly furnished you are.
  —Persius

Have ye not known? have ye not heard? hath it not be told
to you from the beginning?
  —Isaiah 40.21

I shudder and I sigh to think
That even Cicero
and many-minded Homer were
Mad as the mist and snow.
  —W. B. Yeats

A great book is like great evil.
  —Callimachus

I've a great fancy to see my own funeral afore I die.
  —Maria Edgeworth

The sooner every party breaks up, the better.
  —Jane Austen

I am a kind of burr; I shall stick.
  —Shakespeare

It's tough going to costume parties as both ends of the
horse.
  —Anonymous

There is not one among them but I dote on this very absence.
  —Shakespeare

It's tough not to write satire.
  —Juvenal

The more I see of men, the better I like dogs.
  —Mme Roland

If men could give birth, abortion would be a sacrament.
  —Gloria Steinem

May you have a lawsuit in which you know you are in the right.
  —Gypsy curse

Lawyers, I suppose, were children once.
  —Charles Lamb

The law, in its majestic equality, forbids the rich and poor alike to sleep under bridges, to beg in the streets, and to steal bread.
  —Anatole France

I sentence you to hang by the neck until dead.
  —Judicial formula

I will make you shorter by the head.
  —Queen Elizabeth I

If only the Roman people had but one neck.
  —Caligula

A riot is at bottom the language of the unheard.
  —Martin Luther King Jr.

I am the enemy you killed, my friend.
  —Wilfred Owen

Is it possible to succeed without any act of betrayal?
   —Jean Renoir

Never wear a silk shirt to ask for a raise.
   —Anonymous

Luck is the residue of design.
   —Branch Rickey

Don't cheer, men; those poor devils are dying.
   —Rear Admiral "Jack" Philip

Fate is not an eagle, it creeps like a rat.
   —Elizabeth Bowen

Property is theft.
   —Pierre-Joseph Roudhon

Sleep faster, we need the pillows.
   —Yiddish proverb

I see it is impossible for the King to have things done
as cheaply as other men.
   —Samuel Pepys

Good families are generally worse than any others.
   —Anthony Hope

Sir, the insolence of wealth will creep out.
   —Samuel Johnson

It is the wretchedness of being rich that you have to live
with rich people.
   —Logan Pearsall Smith

Every class is unfit to govern.
   —Lord Acton

I have seen the future and it looks just like the present,
only longer.
   —Dan Quisenberry

The ants set an example to us all, but it is not a good one.
   —Max Beerbohm

Let them perish through their own imaginations.
  —The Book of Common Prayer

Every drop of ink in my pen ran cold.
  —Horace Walpole

I know death hath ten thousand several doors
For men to take their exits.
  —John Webster

Pale death kicks through the doors with equal ease
  Of cottages and castles.
  —Horace

Nor bring, to see me cease to live,
Some doctor full of phrase and fame,
To shake his sapient head and give
The ill he cannot cure a name.
  —Matthew Arnold

There is a certain class of clergymen whose mendacity is
only equalled by their mendacity.
  —Archbishop Frederick Temple

I look upon the world as my parish.
  —John Wesley

We have just enough religion to make us hate; but not
enough to make us love one another.
  —Jonathan Swift

Wheresoever the carcase is, there will be eagles gathered
together.
  —Matthew 23.28

Evolutionarily speaking, the development of the anus was
a breakthrough.
  —from a student paper

The nearer the Church the farther from God.
  —Bishop Lancelot Andrews

Even God cannot change the past.
  —Agathon

I was in a printing press in Hell, and saw the method in which knowledge is transmitted from generation to generation.
    —William Blake

If they wanna stay away in droves, you can't stop 'em.
    —Yogi Berra, of baseball fans

A poet's hope, to be,
like some valley cheese,
local, but prized elsewhere.
    —W. H. Auden

There's something I think's better than love, and if you want me to, I'll tell you what it is—that's company.
    —Eudora Welty

Three may keep a secret, if two of them are dead.
    —Benjamin Franklin

A difference of taste in jokes is a great strain on the affections.
    —George Eliot

They make a wilderness and call it peace.
    —Tacitus

Altogether elsewhere, vast
Herds of reindeer move across
Miles and miles of golden moss,
Silently and very fast.
    —W. H. Auden

If you are afraid of loneliness, don't marry.
    —Anton Chekhov

The majority of husbands remind me of an orangutan trying to play the violin.
    —Honoré de Balzac

Set me as a seal upon thine heart, as a seal upon thine arm, for love is strong as death; jealousy is cruel as the grave.
—Song of Solomon 8.6

Never to lie is to have no lock to your door; you are never alone.
—Elizabeth Bowen

I did but taste a little honey with the end of the rod that was in mine hand, and, lo, I must die.
—1 Samuel 14.43

May I ask whether these pleasing attentions proceed from the impulse of the moment, or are the result of previous study?
—Jane Austen

Romance at short notice was her speciality.
—Saki

The credulity of love is the most fundamental source of its authority.
—Sigmund Freud

It is a mistake to think of a bad choice in love, since, as soon as choice exists, it can only be bad.
—Marcel Proust

Everyone is dragged along by his favorite pleasures.
—Virgil

He had often eaten oysters, but had never had enough.
—W. S. Gilbert

"Turbot, Sir," said the waiter, placing before me two fishbones, two eyeballs, and a bit of black mackintosh.
—Thomas Earle Welby

Though sages may pour out their wisdom's treasure, There is no sterner moralist than pleasure.
—Lord Byron

Since I had seen such things depicted in water-colors by
Elstir, I sought to find again in reality, I cherished as
though for their poetic beauty, the broken gestures of
the knives still lying across one another, the swollen con-
vexity of a discarded napkin into which the sun intro-
duced a patch of yellow velvet, the half-empty glass which
thus showed to greater advantage the noble sweep of its
curved sides and, in the heart of its translucent crystal,
clear as frozen daylight, some dregs of wine, dark but
glittering with reflected lights, the displacement of solid
objects, the transmutation of liquids by the effect of light
and shade, the shifting colors of the plums which passed
from green to blue and from blue to golden yellow in
the half-plundered dish, the chairs, like a group of old
ladies, that came twice daily to take their places round
the white cloth spread on the table as on an altar at
which were celebrated the rites of the palate, and where
in the hollows of the oyster-shells a few drops of lustral
water had remained as in tiny holy water stoups of stone;
I tried to find beauty there where I had never imagined
before that it could exist, in the most ordinary things, in
the profundities of "still life."
    —Marcel Proust

There's death in the pot.
    —2 Kings 4.40

The poetry of earth is never dead:
    When all the birds are faint with the hot sun,
    And hide in cooling trees, a voice will run
From hedge to hedge about the new-mown mead.
    —John Keats

If you believe Cratinus, that hoary authority,
and Maecenas, I think you do,
no poems can please for long nor long endure
if they're written by drinkers of water.
    —Horace

Is not a patron, my Lord, one who looks with unconcern
on a man struggling for life in the water, and, when he
has reached ground, encumbers him with help?
   —Samuel Johnson

Nobody ever became depraved overnight.
   —Juvenal

They say someone has taste because he has other
people's taste.
   —Francis Picabia

Oh, life is a glorious cycle of song,
A medley of extemporanea;
And love is a thing that can never go wrong,
And I am Marie of Roumania.
   —Dorothy Parker

My son, may you be happier than your father.
   —Sophocles

      This fell sergeant, death,
Is swift in his arrest.
   —Shakespeare

Wit is the epitaph of an emotion.
   —Nietzsche

I hate quotations.
   —Ralph Waldo Emerson

Shut up, he explained.
   —Ring Lardner

You have delighted us long enough.
   —Jane Austen

Silence is become his mother tongue.
   —Oliver Goldsmith

The Soul of Brevity

As for the aphorism, the maxim, the wisecrack, the Bartlett's entry, the epigram (with, as Martial had it, a sting in its tail), they have their places. They're portable and memorable, and none of us wishes literature were longer or heavier.

Good ones give us the pleasing, if illusory, sense that something has been said right, for once and for all. They have the last word, at least for awhile.

But when a good epigram seems most conclusive—and a good one is nearly all conclusion—and thus most fixed and certain, it is most volatile.

"One's real life is often the life that one does not lead," wrote Oscar Wilde, who built into his witticism the instability of *often*. A reader first concurs with Wilde because he has said it well, and because, after all, he said so many things well it would be a likely mistake not to linger thoughtfully with his sentence. "How often?" a thoughtful reader might wonder, exercising a wary and amused skepticism like the one that prompted Wilde. Little has been concluded and much begun.

A very alert reader might even discover in this particular aphorism a Best in Show example of a characteristic Wilde trope. "Only a man with a heart of stone could read the death of Little Nell without laughing," Wilde quipped, simply substituting *laughing* for the anticipated *weeping* and thus offering a more psychologically acute sketch of the insensate heart. But that wisecrack is easy, especially for Wilde. Saying the opposite of what's usual in "One's real life is often the life that one does not lead" is wiser by far, and Wilde's practiced formula—the reversal of the expected—fills up with wry and provoking ambiguity.

From *The Bread Loaf Anthology of Writers on Writing* (Middlebury, Vt.: Middlebury College Press, 1991).

Of course there are aphorisms that pull shut like doors. "Three may keep a secret, if two of them are dead" (Benjamin Franklin).

Some depend on their context. What compilation of quotations is complete without Emerson's "I hate quotations"?

Others depend on being lifted from context. I found this sentence in an Elizabeth Bowen novel: "Fate is not an eagle, it creeps like a rat." And the retired relief pitcher Dan Quisenberry was quotable enough that there were usually reporters around his locker waiting for something like this: "I have seen the future and it looks like the present, only longer."

And there are aphorisms that depend on forgotten contexts for the ways they are commonly misremembered. Ulysses' famous "One touch of nature makes the whole world kin" (*Troilus and Cressida* 3.3) is usually quoted as a lofty sentiment. But in its original context it is part of Ulysses' attempt to rouse sulky Achilles from his tent, for the fickle world has forgotten what Achilles can do and has the name of Ajax on its every tongue.

> One touch of nature makes the whole world kin—
> That all, with one consent, praise new-born gawds,
> Though they are made and molded of things past,
> And give to dust, that is a little gilt,
> More laud than gilt o'er-dusted.
> The present eye praises the present object.

"What," Ulysses is asking Achilles, "have you done for us lately?"

Whatever incites us to misremember Ulysses' shapely line a nobler context needs deflating, and that's motive enough for a whole class of epigrams.

Bishop Lancelot Andrewes: "The nearer the Church the farther from God."

Or here's one of Martial's acid poems saying exactly what the Roman patronage system rewarded clients to suppress. The poem is number 12, 40, and the translation is mine.

> You lie and I concur. You "give"
> A reading of your wretched verse
> And I applaud. You sing and I
> Too lift my blowsy voice.

You drink, Pontificus, and I
Drink up. You fart; I look away.
Produce a cribbage board; I'll find
a chance to lose, to pay.

There's but one thing you do without
me and my lips are sealed. Yet not
a minim of your money's trickled
down to me. So what?

You'll be good to me in your will?
No doubt you'd bounce a check from hell.
So don't hold back on my account;
If die you must, farewell.

    The best epigrams, like the endings of great poems, shimmer and twist. Little is ended. There's much to think and feel. The rhetorical pleasure of an epigram may be its conclusiveness and concision, but the soul of its brevity is a long thoughtfulness.

    "If you are afraid of loneliness, don't marry," Chekhov wrote. If the reader stops where the rhetorical momentum does, this wisecrack requires no Chekhov. Two guys and some beer will do. But Chekhov is friendlier to loneliness than the lazy reader thinks and friendlier to marriage.

    "Wit is the epitaph of an emotion," wrote Nietzsche, but it would be dull to mistake him as arguing against the chill of wit on behalf of emotion's heat. An emotion has a natural lifespan, and in order for a next one to come along the incumbent needs a death and an epitaph. Of course, reading Nietzsche is not for one who thinks wit and emotional life are different.

    And it will take a very good reader indeed to match wits and emotions with Callimachus: "A great book is like great evil."

Sad Stories and True

Here are the words to Cavaradossi's aria "E lucevan le stelle" from the third act of *Tosca*. The translation is William Weaver's.

And the stars were shining . . .
and the earth was perfumed,
the gate of the garden creaked . . .
and a footstep grazed the sand . . .
She entered, fragrant,
she fell into my arms.
Oh! sweet kisses, oh languid caresses,
while I impatient
freed the beautiful form from its veils!
My dream of love
vanished forever . . .
the hour has fled,
and I die in despair . . .
and I die in despair!
And I have never loved life so much . . .
life so much . . . !

Next, according to the stage directions, Cavaradossi bursts into tears; the aria has reliably had the same effect on me for thirty years.

Cavaradossi believes, and rightly, as it turns out, that he has less than an hour to live, yet it's that hour in the garden he uses the beginnings of his last hour to mourn. "L'ora e fuggita," he sings, but the intensity of that remembered hour brings him both to despair and to the most intense love of life he can imagine.

It's possible to be brought to the brink of such intense feeling, I've found, by full rushes of memory, but if I were at the corner of Eighth Avenue and Nineteenth Street, let's say, and burst first into the aria and then into tears, I'd clear a rather large space around myself. My fellow New Yorkers would recognize me as a street crazy.

For Cavaradossi it's another matter; people do such things in operas, and, besides, the poor bastard has but an hour to live. It's the elaboration of the form—signaling a considerable distance from street life—and the lurid melodrama that release the feeling.

Setting the dates and signing the singers for that performance probably took two years. The singers were flown in from an aggregate twenty thousand miles. The *Tosca* sets were fetched from storage, details of lighting and blocking planned, rehearsals worked through. There are some human emotions—central and powerful ones—it's a major project to release.

In "Sad Stories Told in Bars: The 'Reader's Digest Version' " there is, for a fourteen-line poem, considerable work teasing the emotion out. The low-life setting and expectations of self-pity raised by "Sad Stories Told in Bars," the allusion to the middle-brow *Reader's Digest* that literary folks love to despise and the somewhat mandarin Italian sonnet form all provide, in the tiny way of poems, some distance from the poignancy of the poem's argument, and the tone, veering from falsely jaunty to pluckily morose, suggests the speaker has considerable self-consciousness. But for all that he's in dead earnest.

Maybe that's one of the functions of art, to give us access to emotions so powerful that to consider them all the time would be a mistake: the effort would supplant our routine enjoyment of the world and make Hamlets of us all. But to defer the enjoyment of them—think what pleasure "E lucevan le stelle" can give—until we are, like Cavaradossi, in the literal hour of our death, would be a terrible deprivation.

Privacies

The English word *personal* comes from the Latin *persona*, a mask used by an actor. In its verbal form the word is *personare*, "to sound through." The large-mouthed actor's mask was named from the voice sounding through it.

As for *private*, it comes from the Latin *privatus*, "apart," from the past participle of *privare*, "to bereave." Both of these are derived, according to Skeat, from *privus*, "single, lit. put forward, sundered from the rest." The sense of loss in the Latin is retained in *deprive* and *privation*.

In the army is it better to be a "private" in a barracks or a "general" alone in his office?

And what about the euphemism *privates*, for genitals, those sloggers in the trenches, those trenches, those doughgirls and doughboys? "Grunts," as they were called in Vietnam?

Chamfort: "Men of letters are often criticized for not going out into society. . . . People expect them to be present at a lottery in which they hold no ticket." But of course men and women of letters go out into society as far as they can without losing track of the way back to the desk. The metaphor is not money but food. Men and women of letters go out into society and then retreat: Binge and fast, binge and fast. I'm not sure which is which.

"Solitude is impracticable, and society fatal," wrote Emerson. Neither assertion is true; sworn together, they make a truth.

"This is known as the problem of the one and the many," my philosophy professor said. "Pronouns," I thought, in my blessed ignorance.

A string of articles going back to one by Henry Littlefield in *American Quarterly* in 1964 have offered an allegorical reading for L. Frank Baum's *The Wizard of Oz*. Baum was a gold standard opponent who admired William Jennings Bryan's "Cross of Gold" speech at the 1896 Democratic National Convention but thought Bryan short of resolve.

Bryan, then, is the Cowardly Lion. The Tin Man represents industrial potential wasted by spurning the silver for the gold standard, and the Scarecrow stands for the abused farmer. The Yellow Brick Road is, of course, the gold standard, and leads to Emerald City, or Washington, D.C., where the wizard is a craven and cynical manipulator of imagery who contrives to give the people what they hope to hear and see. Oz is the abbreviation for the plural of *ounce,* by which gold, like other metals, is measured. What about Toto's name? Can the Munchkins be "little people"? Why are Dorothy's slippers silver in the book, though they're ruby in the movie?

Salmon Rushdie asserts that Baum "named his magic world after the letters 'O-Z' on the bottom drawer of his filing cabinet" (*New Yorker,* 11 May 1992). If this assertion were true, would it necessarily contradict Littlefield's article? Does Littlefield offer us an account of how Baum invented the book, or a reading of it?

Of course in much current critical theory the author does not invent books but is invented by, as it were, the unconscious of a particular historical moment in his or her culture and is the helpless master, like the sorcerer's apprentice, of the books he or she writes. A properly trained critic, on the other hand, can decode in these "texts," as books are shabbily called by such critics, the subliminal cultural prejudices, power configurations, and emblems of gender angst that comprise the magma of literature.

"When you interrogate this text . . . ," a job candidate to the university where I teach began a recent compound sentence. *Interrogate* comes from the Latin *inter,* "between or among," and the Latin *rogare,* "to ask." But what the candidate meant was neither the common ground suggested by *between* or *among* nor the courtesy suggested by *ask.* Perhaps the biggest of the many differences between currently fashionable critical theories and their predecessors is how aggressive a critic now permits himself or herself to be to a poem, a book, whatever's under discussion.

Of course, as in police work, a skillful interrogation is very likely to produce the answers it intends to find. This situation would seem likely to produce as many readings as there are critics and thus to splinter the community of readers into competing privacies.

But the issue for many academic critics is to control the vocabulary with which literature is discussed by a generation or two of students, and the better they do that job the more uniform and dully public the discourse grows.

And of course such critics don't need an author with a hobbyhorse and an allegorical yearning, like Frank L. Baum. Baum did too much of their work for them.

Reading is an evasion, one could say, a back turned to the world. The world is vast, one could go on, and a book small, and so why would one turn a back to the one and a rapt face to the other, if a book weren't a kind of corrective lens, "a criticism," as that lugubrious optician Matthew Arnold had it, "of life"? One sees the world more clearly for having read about it, this argument might go, compressed by not much work into a single paragraph.

But a book is part of the world. Illusion is part of reality. Human artifacts are as much a part of nature as hornets' nests. Privacy is part of social life.

As Robert Benchley observed, "The world is divided into two kinds of people—those who are always dividing the world into two kinds of people and those who are not."

"No girl," somebody quotable (Mark Twain?) said, deriding censorship, "was ever ruined by a book," but that's not true. Girls and boys read to be ruined. I went to the library to be ruined, and it worked, so I went back again and again.

The Saturday afternoon movies at the Mayflower Theater in Troy, Ohio, didn't work, which is surely why our prudent parents left us there to see Guy Madison in *The Charge at Feather River*, 3-D glasses free with the price of admission. But my parents took me now and then to a theater in Dayton that showed foreign films, and there, at a flammable age, I saw Louis Malle's

Les Amants. Jeanne Moreau lay in bed, and a man kissed her, and then the camera stayed on her face while the man slid down her body, out of the frame, and her face slowly and deeply bloomed with a nearly anguished pleasure. Hmmm, I thought.

I listened to music to be ruined. Billie Holiday and Lester Young, Little Richard, Jussi Bjoerling, Victoria de los Angelos, Ralph Kirkpatrick playing Bach. I was a slut for ruin. If I'd been born later, I'd have had an 800 number. Nobody in the house had to yell for me to shut my door or turn the music down. Ruin was private, and music, and reading, and didn't movies unreel in the dark?

The notion that books don't ruin you is like the bromide psychotherapists dispense that sexual fantasies are normal and therefore harmless. Sexual fantasies are normal, of course, even endemic, but to comply with truth-in-advertising requirements *harmless* should be replaced by any or all of the following: *repetitive, exhilarating, dire, playful, mesmerizing, incendiary.*

It isn't true that "poetry makes nothing happen." What Auden meant is that our wishes don't change the world outside the reach of our wishes. But the world inside the reach of our wishes, the self, is the world we mostly live in, if only because we have small power in the other, the one we so casually call the "real" world. And in that inner world, where we mostly live, poetry and its allies—prayers, curses, sexual fantasies and other daydreams, letters, diaries, and all the other members of the chorus—make the music, like an internal weather, to which everything happens.

In that inner world we assiduously cultivate what the social world, with its norms and strictures, calls ruin but which we might accurately call individuation.

Literary criticism is easy to judge, after all. It either leads you usefully into a given text or not. I happened onto Derek Traversi's essays on Shakespeare's problem plays when I had just the right combination of curiosity and ignorance to make hard use of them, and, while it's finally true that I learned to read Shakespeare by reading Shakespeare, I'd not have done it so well, however well that may have been, without Traversi's guidance. My gratitude is now thirty-five years long and sharp as the smell of damp paint.

The impersonations that reading allows are company enough for the privacies of reading and probably more.

The most recently fashionable critical theory is already breaking under the weight of its failures. Among the reasons not to applaud is that another will be along shortly to replace it.

What we might hope for is that it will not be as invasive in its ambition to socialize the reading of literature, as militant against that truculent privacy that is both the method and the outcome of good reading, as the deconstructionists and gender theorists have been. They were, after all, a peculiarly sophisticated northern European version of the fundamentalist ideology that has flourished convulsively around the world.

What we need, as ever, is the deep thrall of privacies, good books and time enough to read them so as to reach the ends of them as slowly as possible. As for our critics and teachers, we should simply turn our backs to them if they don't honor such privacies and leave such men and women, may their tribe decrease, to their joyless perturbations.

People Like Us

When the ox was the gray enemy
of the forest and engine of the plow,
the poor drifted across the fields,
through the sweet grasses and the vile,
and tendered bare bowls at our doors.
We hoarded and they begged. We piled
ricks high with hay and they slept there
like barn-cats or cuckoos.

When we sluiced the maculate streets
with fermenting slops, and strode to our jobs
furred by coal-dust, didn't the poor
punctuate our routines with cries
for alms? Our sclerotic rivers
turned the color of old leather
and the poor fished them anyway
and slept under their bridges.

Now they come surging up the stairs
and up the fire escapes. Open our door
to them and then they're us,
and if we don't we're trapped inside
with only us for company
while in the hall they pray and sing
their lilting anthems of reproach
while we bite our poor tongues.

People Like Us

I wrote what turned out to be an early version of "People like Us" while I was working on *Time & Money* (1995) and published it, under a different title, in *Hubbub,* an excellent magazine in Portland, Oregon. I try not to let a poem get loose before I'm sure I've made of it all I can, but in this case I failed.

These days I store my poems in a computer. I can't compose poems on one, I like to say; this formula may be no more than a sour Luddite pride. It seems to me that poems in the magazines are about 20 percent longer since the computer has been in wide use among poets than they were before, and perhaps I don't compose poems on mine as a prophylaxis against windiness.

In any case, I sent my earlier version into cyber-darkness when I rewrote the poem late in 1995. Keeping my own drafts seems to me both a clutter and a vanity. I'm not sure that comparison of my early version to this one would prove instructive, but it's impossible.

The first stanza seems to take place in rural England, the second in London, and the final stanza in a city rather like the one I live in, New York. Perhaps the eras in which the three stanzas happen are more important than the exact settings, for the poem makes little fuss about identifying those settings.

In the first stanza the industrial revolution feels a long way off. Work means converting forests to tillable fields. There's an odd mixture of tones in the stanza: "the sweet grasses and the vile" has a Book of Common Prayer sound to it, and perhaps I had the phrase *vile bodies* not so much "in mind" as in my memory's ear. A similar tone is struck by *tendered.* On the other hand, *the poor drifted across the fields* calls to mind, now, though not when I rewrote the poem, a scene out of *The Night of the Living Dead.* The word *drifted* suggests snow more than any physical menace. Perhaps the major threat the poor can offer here, as else wherein the poem, is to represent the human cost of the prosperity that the ants in the poem (the poor, then, are the grasshoppers) enjoy. It will be to insulate the ants against this constant reminder that, many years after the era depicted in the first stanzas, suburbs will be built.

The poem has some sound patterns in it that don't quite constitute end-rhyme but which are faintly audible all the same. In the first stanza *doors* and *there* look forward to *poor* in stanza 2 and *door*, again, in stanza 3. In stanza 2 *rivers* has a faint link both to *bridges* and *leather*. And in the third stanza *sing* and *tongues* chime softly. I'll leave the investigation of internal rhyme to the curious reader.

The beginnings of the three stanzas are linked: *When* (st. 1), *When* (st. 2), and *Now* (st. 3). All three stanzas are end-stopped; they're complete units. The sentence that ends each stanza is always longer than the one that ends the previous stanza. If this effect contributes anything to the impression that the poem has grown into its own conclusion, as I think it might, it's the sort of effect that can't be planned. The decisions that produce it are made subliminally. It's possible that one major function of revision is to keep the poet in touch with the poem's possibilities long enough for such subliminal patterning to occur. If so, what went wrong with the early version I published in *Hubbub* may well have been not handling the poem long enough.

Of course, it's possible to handle a poem too much. Then the moment comes when the poem goes inert, like dough kneaded too long, and the poet has handled the poem to death.

I notice that things tend to get paired in this poem: *gray enemy* and *engine, sweet grasses* and *vile, hoarded* and *begged, stacked* and *slept,* and *barn-cats* and *cuckoos* are all from the first stanza alone. *And* appears three times in the second stanza and four in the third. They all refer to a larger yoking together that keeps on not getting made, between the poor and the prosperous, the drifters and the workers, between people like us and those on whose bad fortune our good fortune has been built.

In this context we hear the title as heavily ironic. In ordinary social life the phrase *people like us* is used not only to characterize similarity but also to exclude, and the poem keeps suggesting that the excluded are far more like us than we like to think.

There's a fastidious, precisionist diction running through the poem that I associate, looking at the poem now, with an urge toward tidiness and exclusion: *tendered, maculate, scerotic,* and perhaps *punctuate* and *reproach.* A tonic and uncontrollable messiness also infests the poem: *barn-cats, slops, flaring* (I like its proximity to *fire escapes*), and *bite our poor tongues.* The attachment of the adjective *poor* to the tongues of the silent, prosperous folks unsettled by the messy and vocal poor suggests an identity the poem has been hoping to assert to the speaker all along. It may be a happy irony of the poem that this moment can only happen if the speaker voices it himself, and, once he does, the poem's work is over.

The Precisions of Passion

"The vocal instrument is the most difficult of all because it does not exist," says the legendary operatic tenor Alfredo Kraus. He has just come from teaching a master class at Juillard, and the voice is on his mind. But first there are amenities; Kraus is a courtly man. "Would you like a coffee?" he asks me.

His wife, Rosa, brings the coffee, and Kraus apologizes that it may be too strong. It's delicious. "You must hate American coffee," I suggest. Kraus laughs; he's too polite to say so. "We are not used to it."

When he talks about singing, he puts his natural reticence aside. In what sense does he mean that the voice doesn't exist?

An unplayed piano is a piece of furniture, but a singer's voice has no location until it's in use. And even then the voice a singer hears is not the one an audience hears: a singer hears his or her own voice primarily from inside the cave of the body, and the audience hears the freed voice. "You don't hear your voice as it really is, because there are two sounds mixed—the inside and the outside."

Also, "your voice changes from day to day. You don't know why."

Kraus looks out the window of the apartment, near Lincoln Center, he and Rosa inhabit for the month they will be in New York. First dusk sifts the air. "The light was very beautiful today," he says; "why, then, do you suppose they would color the glass like that?" A closer look reveals the window glass is faintly tinted. Something has been done the wrong way.

Kraus's study of the voice, his sense of how best to preserve his voice, and his carefully structured annual schedule are all part of the central paradox of his professional life: to be fastidious,

---

From *Antaeus* (autumn 1993).

thorough, and careful is the best way to release the youthful romanticism, intensity, and passion of the youthful characters he portrays. It is like the slow work of preparing a firework, painstakingly assembled so that a beautiful bravura rush of grace and light comes forth with all the illusion of effortlessness.

"Singing is the only career in music you can have and not be a good musician," Kraus has often said. But a voice is not enough. "To sing you need [two-beat pause] also a voice."

You need, also, Kraus would say, to know your voice and its limits. Speaking of his youth, Kraus said, "My voice was never splendid, and I knew it. My voice is not of tremendous quality, so wonderful in beauty. But it was a material, and you have to know how to manage it."

Asked how he would describe his voice now, he calls it "not tremendously beautiful, but recognizable and characteristic. It's a light, lyric tenor with a lot of metal in the voice and great facility in the high register." At the word *facility* a phenomenon occurs that happens often in talking with Kraus about the voice: a word appears that refers not only to the voice but also to the technique by which it is deployed. Each thing is a part of the other.

Some part of a singer's dynamic range is part of the voice, but learning to expand and use the range is a matter of technique. "If you're always forte, you don't make colors."

Even the management of the voice is part of the voice. Kraus sings about fifty performances a year and works with a comparatively small repertoire. His light, clear voice and technical mastery make him especially at home in the bel canto repertory: *La Favorita, L'Elsir d'Amore, Don Pasquale, Lucrezia Borgia, Lucia di Lammermoor, I Puritani, La Sonnambula, The Barber of Seville.* In the French repertory he sings *Manon, Werther, Faust, Tales of Hoffman, The Pearl Fishers.* Kraus sings some roles in the Italian-language Mozart operas; he has sung Ferrando in *Cosi fan Tutti* and Ottavio in *Don Giovanni.* He has sung Faust in Boito's *Mefistofele* and frequently sings his two famous Verdi roles, Alfredo in *La Traviata* and the Duke of Mantua in *Rigoletto.*

"It's a risk to sing Puccini, because the orchestra is heavy, and you try to push your voice." Kraus has occasionally sung Rinuccio in the one-act *Gianni Schicci* but has otherwise left Puccini alone after singing *Tosca, La Bohème,* and *Madama Butterfly* a couple times each when he was young. By the time he was in his mid-thirties Kraus was an acclaimed artist and could decline roles with impunity. "As an artist," he says, "you have to have the vanity to say no."

Or, as Leonie Rysanek, at sixty-six one year Kraus's senior and still a formidable singer, put it: "The first word to learn is 'no,' if you want a career."

Such willfulness one must cultivate, Kraus thinks. He had a few days earlier watched the young American tennis star Pete Sampras lose a televised Davis Cup match before a partisan and very vocal French crowd in Lyons. "That was hard," Kraus says, "and not really fair. He had to play against almost everyone in the building. He will have to learn to be fierce."

"The voice is like a tube or a channel," Kraus says. The metaphor is ballistic: the voice takes its shape from the throat that expels it.

"To put every sound in the right position is difficult." The notion that sounds have a place should make sense to anyone who has looked at a score, whether or not the onlooker can read music. In the notation of an ascending octave, let's say, each note is one step higher than its predecessors; together they form a kind of staircase. So a score is not just a convenient way to write down musical instructions; it's also a map of the relative *positions* of the sounds. *Map* reminds us of the limitations of a score—it's two-dimensional, and thus a score has a similar relationship to the sounds it encodes (they come from a three-dimensional tube or channel), as a map has to a globe or to the earth.

There are three further complications to understanding the process Kraus describes.

One is that the voice is moving. It passes through the sounds. We could say it moves by means of them, the way one might pick a path across a streambed by stepping on exposed stones.

The second is that in singing opera you are not just producing sounds; each sound is also part of a word, and the words drive the plot—the intrigues, the probable or improbable twists of fate, and ultimately the emotional lives of the characters, their very destinies. "You have to transmit the word," Kraus insists. It's possible to make glorious sound with slack attention to the words you're singing. Joan Sutherland did it for much of her career, hitting the notes accurately and singing with feeling, but the words were drowned in the long, blurred, never-breaking wave of her melisma.

The third is that the proper position for each sound is partially determined by the sound that came before it and the sound toward which it will travel next. You want to make this voyage by the most technically economical and least arduous path possible. The situation could be compared to the difference between expert and inept billiards players. The expert plans each shot to leave the cue ball in the best position for the next several shots. The tyro blasts away and waits to see where the cue ball will stall and only then plots his next move.

Plots seems the right verb, since singing opera is a narrative, a story of what it feels like to be under great emotional pressure. Thus his lifelong fascination with technique. "Emotion," Kraus likes to say, "is a part of our intelligence."

The circumstances under which an international star like Kraus performs are largely influenced by market conditions and thus have changed considerably during his career.

"In Europe we used to have *maestro concertante* and *direttore d'orchestra*—two different things," Kraus recalled in an *Opera News* interview with Edwin Newman. "*Concertare* means 'to put together' . . . all the people who participate in an opera." Sometimes this would entail as much as a week of rehearsal using only the piano. "How to do the recitatives, how to go to a high note and make it *piano,* how to do a *diminuendo,* the feeling, the meaning—they tried to explain everything to us."

Competition for big names that will guarantee a full house and continuous improvement in the technology of air travel have combined to tempt star singers to vault from opera house to opera house. But if you sing in two different cities on successive nights, Kraus warns, "your subconscious is working in two places, and it's too busy."

There are other dangers to this practice. There's never a single way to do an opera. There need to be many, depending on the conductor, the cast, the qualities and limitations of their voices, which of the singers are also actors, etc. If the principals have too little time together, what results can be professional but superficial.

Opera-goers who heard both Kraus and Luciano Pavarotti sing Nemorino in the Metropolitan Opera's production of *L'Elisir d'Amore* in late 1991 had a chance to see how casting choices change an opera to produce quite different and equally credible experiences of it.

Pavarotti is both a charismatic superstar and an extravert. He doesn't immerse himself in a character so much as he inhabits one. It's not only the beautiful bloom of his voice that reminds us that he's in there. Even his stage business suggests not only that he's enjoying playing Nemorino, but also that he's enjoying being Luciano Pavarotti. Nemorino is a credulous bumpkin, greatly the world's fool. Pavarotti's aggressive charm underlines the gap between the character's view of the world and the world's view of him.

Kraus's is an aristocratic temperament and would not permit him the little sob that Pavarotti built into *Una furtiva lagrima*, Nemorino's tender second-act aria. Kraus's reticence and tastefulness predispose him to play well characters whose emotions are implied; his Nemorino suggests by a credulous manner his reserve of clear-hearted dignity. So Kraus's Nemorino is a little nobler than the world he moves in, and, when he sings the role, the force and persistence of his love for Adina seems the central engine of the plot. Kraus's more restrained portrayal makes the opera more romantic.

When Pavarotti sings the role, the social comedy of the opera, the gap between how the characters understand themselves and how we see them, is more central. The love potion is self-delusion, not so much a failing as a social lubrication.

Kraus greatly prefers live performance to recordings. It's not only that studio recordings are often made out of sequence and then cobbled together in the editing room, like a movie. It's also that a performance is a conspiracy, the creation of an atmosphere between performers and audience. "A record is something dead," Kraus says, leaning forward in his chair for emphasis, "because it's repeatable."

Kraus may be right that the audience doesn't always realize when it has been given a superficial performance, but audiences have a subconscious, just as singers do. Sometimes the quality of attention an audience pays to a performance is an eloquent instance of how alert that subconscious can be.

Performers know that there are different kinds of silence from an audience. There is a kind of rapt intensity, like a stretched rope, that only great performances can compel. There are of course varying degrees of attention in the middle range, and at the bottom of this scale there is an inert and inattentive torpor, a kind of mental slouching and bad posture, that all performers dread: it means you might as well be addressing a stableful of dead horses.

The roles to which Kraus has limited himself, in careful stewardship of his voice are often light, lyrical, and uncomplicated emotionally. He has spoken with admiration, and a faint undertow of melancholy, of roles like Otello that must be sung by heavier-voiced and more "heroic" tenors (Placido Domingo and Jon Vickers are the recent prototypes).

But Kraus's career is heroic. He has treated himself as a diligent musician rather than a *divo*. He has treated his audience as an accomplice. He has treated the music he sings as a river that, thank God, it is not possible to cross the same way twice. He continues to teach because he continues to be a student.

"Everything came together," he said once after a particularly soulful and intelligent performance of *La Traviata*. "Everyone came together, and that doesn't often happen." A near grin, a kind of deliberate false start, rippled across his mouth at *always*. Understatement was at work. The perfectionist was almost happy.

Photographs of Nude Women

The comparison of the beloved's body to landscape has been to lyric poetry what the chord changes to "I Got Rhythm" were to bebop. Perhaps the comparison is rooted in childhood? Think of the huge women sculpted by Henry Moore. The adult Moore is in about the same proportion to those massive figures as a nursing infant to its mother's, her swales and meadows. If all new love is old love in disguise, as psychoanalysis and mystics insist, the experience of another's body as landscape is a recapitulation of a first, crucial, irretrievable love.

There is of course a great tradition of photographic nudes that carries into the new medium the centrality of the nude to sculpture and painting. The first of these pictures were deliberately, and necessarily, derivative of painting and sculpture: the new kid needed a lineage. But now, in the time of Lee Friedlander's *Nudes* (1991), to cite a recent collation by a master, the "high art" tradition of the photographic nude has been influenced by—excited by, repelled by, complicated by—pornographic and fashion photography, by pictures frankly contrived to manipulate a willing viewer.

Also, "art" photography can share with the glitziest fashion photography an urge to turn women's bodies into instances of design. "Have you ever noticed how many photographs do nudes that look like peppers?" Ingrid Sischy asks in her "Afterword" to Friedlander's *Nudes*.

In fashion photography there are hand models, ankle models, navel models (navels that resemble tortellini are favored), earlobe models, etc. In the code such pictures and their viewers share, the part readily stands for the whole. These photographs are neither about women nor about looking. They're about commerce, and the fragmentation of the body they effect and trade on seems to me interestingly parallel to the invention of the "department store," a profound leap into the erotics of marketing from "the dry goods store."

The Balkanization of the female nude that two important subgenres of photography, fashion photography and pornography, made possible is institutionalized by the layout of the department store. Perfume and jewelry on the ground floor, lingerie up one, then sportswear, and on up to what used to be called "better dresses." Above that, kitchen and bath items, and still further up, solid bourgeois furniture. There's a sad narrative of a woman's social career here. On the top floor? The credit department, run by a man.

But that last sentence is morally melodramatic. Fashion photography and high-gloss merchandising are two industries in which there are comparatively high percentages of powerful women.

The mall, which has eclipsed the department store, has taken the jerrymandering of the consumer to its logical extreme. *Just Sox* is not only a merchandising scheme but a way to think about one's body without thinking about time. The mall has of course reduced the department store's implied narrative of a woman's social career to a series of snapshots and shrunk the seven (?) ages of woman to three: youth, passing youth along (maternity shops), and fending off all else.

Friedlander's *Nudes* includes few (ten of eighty-five) photographs that show an entire body. The power of the photograph to crop and focus not only the subject but also our attention is routinely employed and in itself offers no conscious or unconscious hostility toward women's bodies. Two things give Friedlander's pictures the humanity so much pornographic and fashion photography has carefully leeched from their preferred images of nude women.

One: taken together, the bodies don't imply a beautiful norm but an interesting diversity of shapes.

Two: these bodies belong to women who live in time and through whom time runs its fierce, lovely current. Puckers and shadows abound. As it happens, Madonna is the model for four of the pictures (1979–80, when she may well have had at least two names). "She wasn't well-groomed," Bob Guccione Sr., the publisher of *Penthouse,* complained of her in these photographs; "there was lots of hair on her arms and hair sticking out of her armpits."

This is a charge Henry Moore would not make about his mother.

Miss Bishop

In those days—1970, 1971?—it was not widely decried as shameful that the editorial board for the distinguished Wesleyan University Press poetry series was four men. Soon it would be decried and even corrected. Such changes have two paces. One is mineral and geological: the slow grinding of subterranean forces. The other, visible one happens while you're out of the room: you come back, and it's no longer smoke filled, and half the voices you hear are women's.

But four men we were: Richard Wilbur, Louis Simpson, John Malcolm Brinnin, and I, a rather timorous young Turk.

Three times a year we'd convene at the press offices in the late morning, work for a while, break for a lunch of sandwiches sent in by a nearby deli. At one such meal Brinnin mentioned Elizabeth Bishop. "I love her work," I said, "an inch short of idolatry, give or take two inches." Brinnin brightened. She was his friend as well as a poet whose work he adored.

Three years later I spent a year in the Boston area teaching. One day the phone rang. It was John Brinnin, who reminded me of that conversation over chicken salad sandwiches and invited me to Duxbury to have drinks and dinner with Miss Bishop.

I was in those days that dreaded thing, a serious young literary man, a sort of bad summer stock St. Paul. So if I'd been John Brinnin, I'd have been a lesser one than he, for I'd not have invited me anywhere. That day thrill ran through me like kind lightning. Of course I'd be there. Thank you, thank you.

The invitation was for five o'clock. I had a class to teach that afternoon, and, by the time it would be done, Boston traffic would be sludge. But I could be there by six. "We'll be having drinks," John said, "and glad to see you when you can get here."

From the *Gettysburg Review* 5, no. 1 (winter 1992).

Though I slithered out of class fifteen minutes early, traffic was a tar pit. I got there at 6:20.

Drinks were in session. Miss Bishop had of course been warned that a young admirer was coming, and she turned her exact attentions to me. She was relaxed, but her focus was intense. "If you didn't have to teach," she asked me almost at once, "would you?"

The prospect was so hypothetical I'd never thought of it. I was rather imploded in those days and said something about the utility of being called out of myself by teaching.

"Ho," she said, and talked with real passion about what in academic life she didn't like—almost everything except what happened in the classroom. At one point I lost a sentence or two while I was berating myself for being so stiff, for being unable to complain accurately about my job just because I was so glad to have it—"and they prefer answers to questions," she was saying with a wry but conclusive tone.

She leaned back in her chair, and we exchanged a few more sentences, and then Miss Bishop, sometimes a heavy drinker in those years, closed her eyes and passed out.

Her companion, Alice Methfussell, turned to me and said, quite sweetly, "Miss Bishop would like to sleep now."

Nurse Sharks

Since most sharks have no flotation bladders and must swim
to keep from sinking, they like to sleep in underwater caves,
wedged between reef-ledges, or in water so shallow
that their dorsal fins cut up from the surf.
Once I woke a nurse shark (so named because it was
thought to protect its young by taking them
into its mouth). It shied from the bubbles I gave up
but sniffed the glint the murky light made on my regulator.

My first shark at last. I clenched
every pore I could. A shark's sense of smell
is so acute and indiscriminate that a shark crossing
the path of its own wound is rapt.
Once a shark got caught, ripped open by the hook.
The fisherman threw it back after it flopped
fifteen minutes on deck, then caught it again
on a hook baited with its own guts.

Except for the rapacious great white
who often bites first, sharks usually nudge
what they might eat. They're scavengers and like
food to be dead or dying. Move to show you're alive
but not so much as to cause panic: that's what the books
advise. The nurse shark nibbled at my regulator
once, a florid angelfish swam by, the shark
veered off as if it were bored. Its nibbled skin
scarped my kneecap, no blood
but the rasped kneecap pink for a week.

Another year I swam past a wallow of nurse sharks asleep
in three feet of water, their wedge-shaped heads lax
on each other's backs. One of them slowly thrashed

its tail as if it were keeping its balance in the thicket
of sharks sleeping like pick-up-sticks. Its tail sent
a small current over me, a wet wind.
I swirled around a stand of coral and swam
fast to shore, startling the sharks to a waking frenzy:
moil, water opaque with churned-up sand,
grey flames burning out to sea. Last time I go diving
alone, I promised myself, though I lied.

"Nurse Sharks"

1. How did the poem start?

Almost always my poems begin with a small scrap of language—a few words or an image. There were two scraps for "Nurse Sharks": the word *wallow* and the image of sharks lying on each other like pick-up sticks. Divers who have spent a hundred times more hours than I have in the water say that they dive because the world they enter is strange. No matter how well you come to know it, it isn't your world: you live in air. In a strange world things are not like themselves, because the first way we know strange things is by comparing them to things we already know. The sharks being more like pigs or pick-up sticks than sharks seemed close to the strangeness of being underwater. I was already in the poem.

Another way we deal with what is strange is to accumulate facts. So in two ways, I must have sensed, the poem I had only two scraps from was going to be about curiosity, among other things.

There is this curiosity about the strange, the other, that makes me want to dive. This is a curiosity about possible experience. I might go into the water and be among sharks.

Then there is curiosity for information. I might read a lot about sharks, and what I learn could help me be among sharks if I go into the water. Or it could just be part of the information I accumulate, like a pack rat, more because I love to gather such things than because I imagine very clearly how I'd ever use them.

A lot of what I've just described happens intuitively, far more quickly, and by a process far more trial and error, than it sounds when I describe it retrospectively.

From *50 Contemporary Poets: The Creative Process,* edited by Alberta Turner (Oberlin, Ohio: Oberlin College Press, 1977).

The sharks' restlessness, his aimless slow circulation seems to advertise by withholding it how much force he has, how at home he is in the water that is strange to us. When I first learned that most sharks have no flotation bladders, I wondered immediately how they slept. I imagined an exhausted shark sinking deeper into sleep and into deeper, blacker water. I was curious to learn what I could about shark behavior, and I wanted to learn from people who had studied shark behavior long and exactingly enough that they didn't anthropomorphize the shark. But it was the legends about sharks I hoped my shark book would explode that had led me to read the book. And I was already using the metaphors of science to augment my own metaphors. I'd imagined as insomniac shark.

Besides, there is no such thing as "the shark." There are individual sharks, members of distinct species.

I wanted the poem to move by this kind of thinking—assertions and corrections—that resembled the tentative diver's curiosity.

2. What changes did it go through from start to finish?

As usual, I took out a few lines during my last revision. I wrote "Nurse Sharks" quickly, with one large revision (described in the next section) between first draft and final revision, which often, for me, is like the step described in cookbooks by "Correct for seasoning." Often in an early draft of a poem I say things that, it turns out as I go along, are apparent without me saying them. They're said by implication, or by the poem's pace or shape, and so don't need to be explicit. Such lines are notes to myself. I may have needed them to write the poem, but the poem didn't need them. Its needs and mine are always different. The better the negotiations between them, the better the poem.

3. What principles of technique did you consciously use?

Most of my technical decisions in writing a poem are made intuitively, the way a basketball player puts a higher arc on his shot when he senses an opponent will jump high enough that the usual arc would result in the shot being blocked. Such decisions are neither conscious nor unconscious. I suspect they're both.

But if we take "conscious" decisions to mean those we make very deliberately, rather than so swiftly we don't know exactly how they're made, I made such a decision, important to the poem and startling to me. In its first finished draft the poem was in shorter lines. The first line read and the lines, though they varied in length, were as much shorter through the poem as that first line is than the first line of the finished poem. The first version was too choppy. I had written it the way it stood in the first draft more from habit—the length of the first line in the first draft is a comfortable and supple length for me—than the good negotiation between the poem's needs and mine. My needs—they turned out to be false needs—were to do it in a way I'd already learned, i.e., to be lazy. The poem needed longer lines to accommodate the relaxed, discursive pace I'd use in giving much shark data. The apparent antagonists in the poem are "I" and some nurse sharks. They turn out to be false antagonists, as do the fact-gathering and the experience-gathering curiosities of "I." I needed the longer line to make this second false antagonism have the right weight in the poem.

It was the first time I'd ever made such a revision throughout a poem, but I went back and lengthened the lines; then I made a few small changes required by the new lineation. The poem was better for it.

4. Whom do you visualize as your reader?

Nobody. I know there will be readers, but I can't know who they will be. Or, a second possible answer, also true. I visualize as my reader a me who somehow wasn't present when I wrote the poem and can thus read it as if it were written by somebody else. But this imaginary creature is as plausible as an insomniac shark.

5. Can the poem be paraphrased? How?

No. To use different language is to say something different. I called the angelfish "florid" because angelfish are brightly colored, like tropical flowers. And because *florid* is often used to describe someone's complexion, and a pink kneecap comes into the poem shortly after the angelfish. And also because *florid* suggests being short of breath, excited, flustered. I could say more about *florid* or any word in the poem. It's not only what a word does in its own place in the poem but how it bounces and echoes off other words. The poem isn't more than the sum of its parts. A sum is still. A poem is more than the *activity* of its parts. If it's alive, you not only can't paraphrase it; you can't even change a word.

6. How does this poem differ from earlier poems of yours in (a) quality, (b) theme, (c) technique?

a. It's better than most of them. Or, I like it more. In an important way the comparison is impossible. Presuming that I write as well as I'm able at any given time in my writing life, I can turn from a poem and say it's "bad," but not because I am. I was more curious than capable. But I can write "good" poems easily by writing poems I've already learned to write. If I am not writing as well as I'm able, that's another question altogether.

b. I don't think interesting poems have themes. To say to a student that some poem is "about illusion and reality" is to give the student a first and very crude way to think about the poem. That's fine, if it leads into the poem: words, silences, rhythms. But if the idea "theme" becomes a place to stop and look and go no further, like a "scenic overlook" at a park, then it's a useless idea. You have to go in.

c. After a poem is finished, technique is how it was done. While poems are being made, it's hard to say anything exact enough to be interesting about technique. It's a kind of responsiveness, really, an alertness to the poet's energies and possibilities. A crucial part of it, then, is one's own writing experience, accumulated. A larger part of it is what a poet can learn from others—teachers, contemporaries, the great masters of the past. Indeed, anyone who has helped give the language the shape in which it comes to us. Perhaps technique is an active love of the language.

Sentimental Villainy

High-mindedness is not curiosity.

It may have led us to our widespread, current assumption that a beaver lodge is one of the wonders of nature but that human dwellings are somehow separate from nature and probably poisonous to it.

When Emerson came to the Adirondacks in August 1858, he felt a strong dichotomy.

> Look to yourselves, ye polished gentlemen!
> No city airs or arts pass current here.
> Your rank is all reversed; let men of cloth
> Bow to the stalwart churl in overalls:
> They are the doctors of the wilderness,
> And we the low-prized laymen.

The "they" of whom Emerson wrote were native guides and the "polished gentlemen" his Boston friends.

The organizer of the excursion was William James Stillman (1828–1901), at various times a painter (he studied landscape painting with Frederick E. Church), a journalist, an outdoorsman, and a diplomat (U.S. consul to Rome in 1861–65 and to Crete in 1865–69). He was a variously able man who never chose one ability to pursue full bore.

In 1857 he took some notables from the Boston-Cambridge-Concord axis to the Adirondacks: James Russell Lowell, Lowell's brother-in-law, two of Lowell's nephews, and John Holmes (brother to Oliver Wendell Holmes).

The next summer the group expanded to include Emerson, Louis Agassiz, Judge Hoar (later attorney general in Grant's cabinet). Of the ten only one was not a member of the Saturday

---

First appeared in the *Ohio Review* (1993).

Club. Four belonged to the Whist Club. And they all became, on the sylvan spot, members of the Adirondack Club of Boston.

> The rumor of the advent of the party spread throughout the country around Saranac, and at the frontier town where they would begin the journey into the woods the whole community was on the *qui vive* to see, not Emerson or Lowell, of whom they knew nothing, but Agassiz, who had become famous in the commonplace world through having refused, not long before, an offer from the Emperor of the French of the keepership of the Jardin des Plantes and a senatorship if he would come to Paris and live. Such an incredible and disinterested love for America and science in our hemisphere had lifted Agassiz into an elevation of popularity which was beyond all scientific or political dignity, and the selectmen of the town appointed a deputation to welcome Agassiz and his friends to the region. A reception was accorded, and they came, having taken care to provide themselves with an engraved portrait of the scientist to guard against a personation and waste of their respects. The head of the deputation, after having carefully compared Agassiz to the engraving, turned gravely to his followers and said, "Yes, it's him"; and they proceeded with the same gravity to shake hands in their order, ignoring all the other luminaries.

It was Emerson who most fascinated Stillman.

And Emerson was such a study as can but rarely be given any one. The crystalline limpidity of his character, free from all conventions, prejudices, or personal color, gave a facility for study of the man limited only by the range of vision of the student.

Also in his *Autobiography of a Journalist* (1901) Stillman wrote:

We were ten, with eight guides, and while we were camping there we received the news that the first Atlantic cable was laid and the first message sent under the sea from one hemisphere to the other—an event which Emerson did not fail to record in noble lines.

Stillman had hoped to enlist Longfellow for the trip.

"Is it true that Emerson is going to take a gun?" he asked me, and when I said that he [Emerson] had finally decided to do so, he [Longfellow] ejaculated, "Then somebody will be shot!" and would talk no more of going.

In Stillman's autobiography and other accounts this gathering was called "The Philosophers' Camp," a name that moved Emerson to the center of the group.

How did they pass their time?

In the main, our occupations were those of a vacation, to kill time and escape from the daily groove. Some took their guides and made exploration, by land or water; after breakfast there was firing at a mark, a few rounds each, for those who were rifle-men; then, if venison was needed, we put the dog out on the hills; one boat went to overhaul the set lines baited the evening before for the lake trout. When the hunt was over we generally went out to paddle on the lake, Agassiz and Wyman to dredge or botanize or dissect the animals caught or killed; those of us who had interest in natural history watching the naturalists, the others searching the nooks and corners of the pretty sheet of water with its inlet brook and its bays and recesses, or bathing from the rocks. Lunch was at midday, and then long talks.

Emerson tried to kill a deer but couldn't; his "indifference to the mere form of things," as Stillman characterized it, was perhaps an impediment.

Stillman bought, on behalf of the Adirondack Club of Boston, 22,500 acres for six hundred dollars. The price was low because the tract "had been forfeited to the State at the last tax sale and was for sale at the land office in Albany."

The next summer Stillman was abroad; without his social energies, attendance fell off. Then the Civil War broke out, and the club was done. According to Alfred L. Donaldson's *A History of the Adirondacks* (1921), "it gradually faded into non-existence, and the land reverted to the State for unpaid taxes."

Years later Henry van Dyke found at Ampersand Pond—no pond but a substantial lake—the cabin built as a clubhouse for the Adirondack Club of Boston, tenanted only by an interesting family of what the guides quaintly call "quill pigs" and surrounded by an almost impenetrable growth of bushes and saplings, among which a brood of partridges were in hiding. The roof had fallen to the ground; raspberry bushes thrust themselves between the logs; and in front of the sunken door sill a rusty, broken iron stove, like a dismantled altar on which the fire had gone out forever.

It's all too easy to poke fun at Emerson, of course; nobody's ever been great without being equally silly.

And amiable, star-struck Stillman is an easier target yet. Who was "the Emperor of the French" in 1858? Was everyplace beyond Boston "the commonplace world"? Did French law permit the grant of a "keepership" and a "senatorship" at the whim of American journalists?

All the same, these were urbane, intellectual men who went to the wilderness as tourists.

In an editorial on 9 August 1864, titled "A Central Park for the World," the *New York Times* rhapsodized about the extension of railroad lines into the Adirondacks, northward from Saratoga, "aiming directly at the heart of the wilderness":

> The jaded merchant or financier or litterateur or politician, feeling excited within him again the old passion for nature (which is never permitted entirely to die out) and longing for the inspiration of physical exercise and pure air and grand scenery, has only to take an early morning train in order, if he chooses, to sleep the same night in the shadow of the kingly hills and waken with his memory filled with pleasant dreams, woven from the ceaseless music of mountain streams.

Alongside the jaunty, acquisitive tone of the *Times* editorial, like a shadow, fear of human enterprise abounds in the literature of the Adirondacks. Francis Parkman first went to the area as a college student on vacation. Later he liked to call his life's work "the history of the American forest." Fifty years after that first trip he wrote a friend about what had happened in the meantime.

> The *nouveau riche*, who is one of the pests of this country, has now got possession of the lake and its islands. For my part, I would gladly destroy all his works and restore Lake George to its native savagery.

By such strident tones we can measure the force by which a good heart had been broken.

Robert Marshall, who once ascended fourteen Adirondack peaks in one day, starting at 3:30 A.M. and topping the last one at 10:10 that night, wrote the following about the view, seen on a less hectic day, from Mt. Haystack.

> From Haystack you can look over thousands and thousands of acres, unblemished by the works of man, perfect as made by nature.

There are two good reasons to cordon off huge tracts of wilderness and repel humans as well as you can. One has been soulfully put by Aldo Leopold: "Of what avail are forty freedoms without a blank spot on the map?"

The other, of course, is that humans cause more, greater, and less reparable damage to the balance of life on the planet than any other species and are so suicidally slow to admit to their destructive power that, whenever we can handcuff them, we should. The moral problem in that last sentence is that both *we* and *them* refer to humans.

Here are a few lines from Emerson's "The Adirondacs," capturing the giddy pleasures of the 1858 expedition.

> Lords of this realm,
> Bounded by dawn and sunset, and the day
> Rounded by hours where each outdid the last
> In miracles of pomp, we must be proud,
> As if associates of the sylvan gods.
> We seemed the dwellers of the zodiac,
> So pure the Alpine element we breathed,
> So light, so lofty pictures came and went.
> We trode on air, contemned the distant town,
> Its timorous ways, big trifles, and we planned
> That we should build, hard-by, a spacious lodge
> And how we should come hither with our sons,
> Hereafter—willing they, and more adroit.

There's an unquestioned access in these lines not only to the wilderness but also to the most grandiose emotional states—represented by the religious diction of *lords, miracles of pomp, syl-*

van gods, and *dwellers of the zodiac*—that the wilderness could inspire in Emerson and his friends.

To be a little delirious in the presence of such beauty makes perfect sense. But the grammar of the first sentence in that passage provides another reason, besides the inflated rhetoric, for suspicion: "Lords of this realm, . . . we must be proud." Once the pride has slackened, the camp will sag to ruin and the taxes go unpaid.

If a similar group of worthies today could make such an expedition and have it be so assiduously recorded, the tone would certainly be quite different.

There would be none of Emerson's cheerful patrilineal optimism but, instead, the melancholy frisson of things coming to an end, or at least to the beginnings of an end. Someone would surely say the phrase *a place we haven't ruined yet,* as if nature were where we go to think on what we fell from.

Whatever art we're going to have the rest of our lives, and beyond, had better find a way not to use nature as a whip to scourge ourselves but, rather, imagine how we might live in nature, rather than set ourselves apart from it like wicked children.

It was only a few years after the Philosophers' Club's brief life that Matthew Arnold made, from England, his melancholy prediction that art would replace religion. He was wrong. Nature replaced religion.

Nature had not fared so well under the old dispensation, for was not the very creation fallen? Was not the earthly span of humans a kind of debriefing for the confused soul, at the end of which humans would shuck off their "vile bodies," as *The Book of Common Prayer* calls them, and, like chicks stepping out of their eggs, move to our weightless, immaterial destinations?

But to worship nature we make it bigger, better, far away. God used to be like that, for no slumlord lives in the slums. We have set nature apart from ourselves so easily and readily we speak of "the natural world" without asking ourselves the obvious and necessarily consequent question: What might the unnatural world be? We have come to love nature for what it isn't—tainted by us, its sentimental villains.

This is a dangerously long way from the situation Frost discovers in the beautiful last line of "Hyla Brook."

We love the things we love for what they are.

Hail, Muse! Et Cetera

So Byron jauntily begins canto 3 of *Don Juan*. Later he offers his Muse these guarded instructions:

> March, my Muse! If you cannot fly, yet flutter;
> And when you may not be sublime, be arch,
>   Or starch, as are the edicts statesmen utter.
> We surely shall find something worth research:
>   Columbus found a new world in a cutter,
> Or brigantine, or pink, of no great tonnage,
> While yet America was in her non-age.
>
> (15.210–16)

The comparison of the poem's progress to a voyage of discovery is of course mockingly grandiloquent—surely the central tone of the poem. Byron means to subvene the grandiosity of the epic and to associate its conventionally lofty rhetoric with the banalities of statesmen. But he also means to discover something new—a tone in which a long poem can be written that is resolutely up-to-date and yet can share in the epic's prestige. His own poem he calls "this Epic Satire" (14.790).

Horace is the classical poet he cites most frequently: this fact should remind us what urbanity of tone and range of moral authority Byron aspires to.

Indeed, Byron is so eager to be Horatian that he attributes to Horace a swatch from Ovid:

> In short, the maxim for this amorous tribe is
> Horatian, "Medio tu tutissimis ibis."
>
> (6.135–36).

"You'll fare best on the middle path," Ovid wrote, in *Metamorphoses*, 2.137.

It is indeed a middle path—between the length and grandiosity of the epic and the pointed compression of satire—that Byron has set himself on. Thus Horace is Byron's honorary guide.

But why is Martial so important to Byron's project? He first appears in canto 1, where Byron is detailing Juan's education.

> And then what proper person can be partial
> To all those nauseous epigrams of Martial?
>
> Juan was taught from out the best edition,
>   Expurgated by learned men, who place,
> Judiciously, from out the schoolboy's vision,
>   The grosser parts; but fearful to deface
> Too much their modest bard by this omission,
>   And pitying sore his mutilated case,
> They only add them all in an appendix,
> Which saves, in fact, the trouble of an index;
>
> For there we have them all at one fell swoop,
>   Instead of being scatter'd through the pages;
> They stand forth marshall'd in a handsome troop,
>   To meet the ingenuous youth of future ages,
> Till some less rigid editor shall stoop
>   To call them back into their separate cages,
> Instead of standing staring altogether,
> Like garden gods—and not so decent either.
>
>   (1.343–60)

The garden gods Byron refers to were statues (usually wooden) of Priapus with an exaggerated erection—ribald scarecrows. Much of the diction of this passage (*less rigid, stand forth, grosser parts, modest bard, mutilated*) has been pointedly anticipating this phallic conclusion. For those of Byron's readers who knew what he meant by *garden gods*, the last couplet brings an underground river of snickers to the surface. The effect is rather like that of so many Latin sentences in which the verb is deferred to the very end and organizes both the syntax and the sense of the sentence like a tightened drawstring.

As for the edition Byron has Juan taught from, Byron's commentary on his own poem reads: "Fact. There is, or was, such an edition, with all the obnoxious epigrams of Martial placed by themselves at the end."

Outside literature and the scholarly presentation of it, the sordid and the noble are inextricably braided together.

Two lines of *Don Juan* consist of a Martial epigram quoted whole and Byron's commentary on it. The italics are Byron's.

> Omnia vult *belle* Matho dicere—dic aliquando
>   Et *bene,* dic *neutrum,* dic aliquando *male.*
> The first is rather more than mortal can do;
>   The second may be sadly done or gaily:
> The third is still more difficult to stand to:
>   The fourth we hear, and see, and say too, daily:
> The whole together is what I would wish
> To serve in this conundrum of a dish.
>
> (14.161–68)

Byron doesn't translate Martial's epigram for his readers, just as he didn't tell them in canto 1 what he meant by *garden gods.* Martial's epigram is 10.46. I've translated it as follows:

> Whatever you say, Matho, it's got to be smart.
> There's nothing good, or dull, or evil in your heart?

The stanza could serve as a motto for the whole poem. Byron's complaint about the great epics is their unmixed tones. Grandeur follows on grandeur. Virgil is never not *belle,* which means in Latin (as in modern Italian) not only beautiful but stylishly so, elegant. Likewise, *smart* in modern English points both to modishness and intelligence.

"The first," Byron says, meaning *belle,* "is rather more than mortal can do." Byron has used *mortal* very seriously here. The "mortals" in Homer and Virgil are great heroes. Every male character in *The Iliad* except Thersites is a prince or a king. The gods of course can't die, which is why they're finally trivial, except for their power, and why "mortals" like Achilles are at their most foolish when they're most godlike.

The great epics Byron is both honoring and satirizing are not about mortals, in the ordinary sense of the word, but *Don Juan* is.

Mortals are not all *belle* but good, so-so, and evil all muddled together. To be good, *bene,* provides no unmixed sense of moral victory; it "may be sadly done or gaily." Or, by implication, both at once, with very mixed feelings.

Neutrum, or so-so, or dull, "is still more difficult to stand to," Byron tells us. How so? The translation *dull* suggests why: we're bored by it.

Male is at least dramatic, which may be why we quickly assent to Byron's observation that "we hear, and see, and say [it] too, daily." The rhyme of *gaily* and *daily* is one of the wonders of this stanza. The erosion of the *daily* eats away at the peak-experience sense of life implicit in *gaily.*

And daily life is Byron's subject. His characters exist in time, in contrast to the heroes of the great epics, suspended forever in mythological timelessness.

The ottava rima stanza that Byron chose for his satiric epic provides a loping pace congenial to both his narrative impulses and to his love of digression and commentary:

> I meant to make this poem very short,
> But now I can't tell where it may not run.
>
> (15.171–72)

Byron here is being cheerfully disingenuous. He always intended a very long poem.

> I've finished now
> two hundred and odd stanzas as before,
> That being about the number I'll allow
> Each canto of the twelve, or twenty-four.
>
> (2.1722–25)

Virgil's poem has twelve books; Homer's two poems have twenty-four each. Byron's aim was always to match the epic in scale but to modernize it, to satirize it, to make it about mortals and their daily behavior rather than about heroes and their legendary behavior. He wanted also a tone that represented not just the *belle* but also the mixed feelings and motives of mortals under stress and in confusion.

And he wanted a form that allowed, even demanded, an element of commentary and concision to counterbalance the expansive, digressive, and learned baggage of his authorial journey. So the rhymed couplet that concludes each ottava rima stanza is an opportunity for Byron's epigrammatic instincts, for a series of contractions that counter the expansive chatter of the long, apparently meandering poem.

See what happens in the concluding couplet of the stanza Byron devotes to Martial's epigram.

> The whole together is what I could wish
> To serve in this conundrum of a dish.
>
> (15.167–68)

The idea of a stew (or "mess," to look back to the biblical meaning of *mess of pottage,* which survives into our military diction: *mess hall*), with a little bit of everything in it, derives very exactly from Byron's rejection of the *belle* for the more inclusive range of effects and tones necessary to depict the daily emotional lives of mortals. The muse here is no glowing hologram but kitchen help with gravy stains on her apron.

But if *dish* serves to deflate a certain literary pretension Byron associates with the great epics, *conundrum* serves to elevate *dish* to one of the mysteries and thus to compare it to the mess, the *missa* (as the Mass, that ceremonial meal at which the celebrants eat the body and drink the blood of a god, is called in Latin).

The major strategy of Byron's poem is packed tightly into his stanza on Martial's epigram. I will invite, he seems to be reminding himself, comparison with the great epics. I will differentiate my satirical epic from those great poems by insisting on a complication of tone necessary to display the full range of daily mortal emotion. The resulting mess will be humbler than Homer, or Virgil (or Dante or Milton, models less important to Byron's contrast but by no means ignored by him). But, by being humbler, it will be more accurate about the great human mysteries, which happen not to our heroes but to ourselves.

And accuracy is Byron's goal.

> But if a writer should be quite consistent,
> How could he possibly show things existent?
>
> (15.695–96)

Journal Entries

Entries from two different periods several years apart have been combined here. I heard them in the same key, and so, rather than simply append the later to the earlier, I folded, as cookbooks say, one into the other.

Why do I record these scraps? So that, later, when I've forgot what impulse led me to record them (much of what I keep is written by others—I keep a commonplace book and journal simultaneously) or write them, I can pick them up and see them as if they were freshly found rather than long hoarded.

—WM

"If we could know ourselves, it would be a violation of ourselves."

—Edwin Muir

"*Tsar* and *Kaiser* are both cognates for *Caesar,*" the Latin teacher tells students triumphantly. See how the past survives, the teacher thinks. A mob's a mob the world around, thinks a student. We humans are perhaps at our worst when we think we've got something figured out.

To eavesdrop is an ordeal.
—Elizabeth Bowen

An oxymoron: "Dead language."

A language is communal and historical. It's a river that sweeps the present downstream, out to sea. Parts of any language die all the time. "He was gay," my grandmother says, who wonders why her Lesbian granddaughter had so few "beaux."

A portion of these journal entries first appeared in *The Poet's Notebook* (New York: W. W. Norton, 1995). The remaining entries first appeared in *Seneca Review* 21, no. 2 (1991).

My grandmother means he was mirthful. The language has beached her and swirled ahead. The world—she's ninety-eight—has done the same.

No doubt some languages have died, but we don't know which ones they were.

When we say "dead languages," we mean "the classics"— Greek, Latin, and, for the arcane and scholarly, Sanskrit—which a few of us have assiduously kept alive, the way a few in any generation make genealogical charts.

They may be in zoos, but they're alive.

Still, it may be that what we most value in them is in fact "dead," as fossils are. That *senile* and *Senate* have the same root, *sad* and *sated,* and likewise *wife* and *gift.*

From a student paper on whether entertainers have an obligation to act as role models: "The reason young people don't respect their parents is they're not well known."

Sebastian has sent me a tape from a new release of Bob Dylan bootlegs, so I spend a happy forty-five minutes comparing the versions of "Idiot Wind" I already have with one new to me. I envy the purely private fun it must be to turn one's work inside out, mock it, vamp it, make it both new and continuous with its former versions. A poem in a book is finished; the type is "set."

I realize that I approach my *Selected Poems* with a gravedigger's melancholy but none of the gravedigger's nasty humor. The task feels like exhumation.

It has, I know, nothing to do with whether they're good or not, but I'd like the poems I'll select more if I could treat them the way Dylan does his earlier recordings. Do I stand by them? Of course, even when that pose casts me as a gawky kid with a prom date. What did she see in him, or he in her?

As the Kunitz poem has it, "I only rented this dust." So then comes the moment you have to turn it in. They've already made an imprint of your credit card when you took the dust off the lot. "How much dust," you ask politely, "do I owe you for the use of this dust?"

I may well have on tape every recorded note played by Lester Young. The particles of musical information on each of those tapes are a sort of organized dust.

"I need a rhythm section like old people need soft shoes," said Lester. They wheel it through the gates of the fort. Beautiful carving, beautiful wood. The Trojan Slipper.

So Lester needed a capable rhythm section. One night he got a drummer he'd worked with before, unhappily. They were sitting around after the first set, and the drummer, who sensed that things weren't going well, was making cheerful patter. "Hey," he asked Lester, "when was the last time time we worked together?"
Lester sighed, then said, "Tonight."

Musicians' joke:
Q: What class of people likes to hang around with musicians?
A: Drummers.

Half-rhymes: *by rote, by heart. Dint, ain't. Tell, all. Finish, Spanish. Worst, Proust. Latin, pattern.*

In a bad end-rhymed poem, you can have 80 percent of the available fun by reading only the far right-hand strand of the poem, the beach where the vowels break, and there the plot, the argument, the "paraphrasable content" (but not the poem), the matter (but not the energy), are in swarm, like the bees in this morning's *Times.* The street (East Eighty-second?) had to be closed off. Why were they there? "Apparently the queen had become attached to a white Honda."
In a good end-rhymed poem the bees are everywhere, but the rhymes help you know where you are. First *you* means the poet and then the reader. There is no third person in this grammar.

Soul: A reader? My kingdom for a reader.
Body: The reader can't come to the phone just now, but how about a mirror?

Ali, after his loss to Holmes: "I had the world, and let me tell you, it wasn't nothing."

Body: Why no poems in these notebooks, not even scraps or smithereens? What's the project, after all?

Soul: I'm going to ignore the moronic japery about the project. As for poems, there will be wine from these grapes.

Some employees of the Federal Reserve Bank wear magnesium shoes to protect their toes against dropped gold ingots.

Bread Loaf lecture coming up. . . . How many odd rhetorical forms and feints I've devised over the years to avoid writing a conventional essay, in which, like a sheepdog, the author jollies along a flock of argument.

It's always a writer who thinks of himself as a realist, in the relationship he covets between his work and the texture of experience, who will say to me, quizzically, after I've read the piece, "It was fascinating, but what exactly did it mean?"

There's a rage for meaning, to be sure. Freud's work, in which every retrievable scrap of dream and slip of the tongue are wrung like precious sponges for meaning, may be the great, mad, tragic text on rage for meaning. What did he find? A blurry snapshot. So who benefits? We do, for we have his writings, a great emotional document.

> Most of my life has been spent not understanding, and
> I can assure you, it was not easy.
>
> —Rilke

You can abandon your own poem at any point, not so much because it's done, but because seven hundred calories, or seven thousand, of additional energy spent on it wouldn't produce, you judge, proportionate improvement. On to the next, you decide; they're your poems, and it's your energy. And you're not done, either.

But Martial's been done since A.D. 104. What right do you have to abandon that epigram that even Dudley Fitts or Rolfe Humphries or James Michie or Fiona Pitt-Keithley didn't quite get right, or so you suspect the more strongly the longer you too fail to get it right?

You have every right. You're just a minnow, and Martial's a mullet, but he's dead, and you're not.

Translation's a problem in English. In the first sentence of this year's Bread Loaf anti-lecture I use the word *gaud*, but in my Southwestern Ohio dialect it will sound like *god* or, worse, *God*, and in order to read it aloud without wrongly causing puzzlement or hurt I'll need to frontload, as the mutual fund salespeople say, the talk with an explanation.

"It's all material, I know . . . ," I heard a writer begin a sentence that listed a deluge of grief and death and betrayal that would make Job burst like a boil. Living in the material world . . .
It's pain. The meaning of pain is pain.

> Regret is the fruit of pity.
> —Genghis Khan

How private is a journal if some entries get published? Who's this written for? What does it mean to sing in the shower? If a shower falls over on a desert island . . . ?

If you write it, it's not private. Scholars and, of course, lawyers believe this. I once heard a lawyer, not mine, say, "It's our position that this piece of paper doesn't exist."

> This is my curse. *Pompous,* I pray
> That you believe the things you say
> And that you live them day by day.
> —J. V. Cunningham

Epitaph: Was I right or what?

Sibelius, asked the meaning of his fourth symphony: "Play the record again."

"I think your poem doesn't take enough risks," one kind of workshop student will say. But nobody ought to be allowed to visit that kind of moral blackmail on a fellow student. The teacher should require the assailant to say exactly what kinds of risk and exactly where in the poem they should be taken and exactly where his or her gall and boorishness came from.

To get out of her house for a while, my grandmother asked me to take her for a drive around the small village she's lived in all but twenty of her ninety-five years. "The Lovetts' house once," she'd say. "No more."

Another house: "Martin Mortimer's place. Three wives."

"What was he like?" I asked.

"Dreadful snob," she said.

Another house. "Handsome Don Ransom's house," she said.

"What did he look like?"

"A chipmunk."

You get old; you hoard your verbs.

Of course, if you were born in 1896, your world has shed its skin five times or six, and you're the oldest person you've actually met. When was the last time you dreamed of anyone still alive?

Rebuild. Retool. Remarry. Change your life. Do we index that last one under *Life, you must change your,* or under *Change your life, you must?* Why, whenever I hear that half-line of Rilke quoted, always solemnly, do I wonder how large a diaper I'll need?

Gossip: a way to afflict the sadness you fear on others. Or, even sadder than that, the happiness you fear.

One lure of gossip consists in how much work it takes, and how enjoyable that is, to change the known world to fit a theory about it. ("But if she's recently inherited money and doesn't want us to know about it, that would explain. . . .") In that way gossip resembles detective fiction or most literary criticism.

Gossip: I know it's true; I heard it from you.
Art: You know it's true; you heard it from me.

> He left as rose behind her head,
> A meat axe in her brain.
> A note upon the bureau read:
> "I won't be back again."
> —Raymond Chandler

More from Chandler:

1. If you don't leave, I'll find somebody who will.
2. I left her with her virtue intact, but it was quite a struggle. She almost won.
3. Goodnight, goodbye and I'd hate to be you.

Exit lines, ends of paragraphs, ends of chapters: Chandler was the imprisoned master of the last word.

Why do I read that stuff? The rusted slang, the clumsy expositions ("I turned west on Pico, but I couldn't shake a dozen unanswered questions that stayed on my tail"), the mushheart-toughguy imitations of Samuel Johnson (*Hammett:* "The gaudier the patter, the cheaper the hood"), the snakes-with-their-bad-tasting-tails-in-their-mouths plots, the slinky and untrustworthy heiresses played by Bette Noir, the stripes and shadows of black-and-white like plaster and lath. . . .
(Does Pico run west?)
Describing why I ought not to like it, I have perhaps made it sound more attractive than it is, like a smoker talking about not being able to quit.

A yellow dress, a crusted spoon, an un-watered begonia? The clue's only one scrap in the world's rich litter and since you don't know what it is nor how to guess you're driving west on Pico, low on gas and snappy patter. Moral dusk again for the romantic loner: good doesn't count until there are others, and then it's impossible. . . .

Grace under Pressure

There's no other kind: pressure makes it
grace or else it's charm, as in *charm bracelet.*

The Poet's End

He paled, he wrote more poems, white heat,
etc. Then he grew worse.
The grand tour to the last resort
often leaves an exhaust of verse.

Death is the mother of beauty? No doubt. Also of blackmailers, debutantes, baggers of groceries, corrupt cops, babies, funeral directors, and all the shrinks who live in, or rent office space in, the building on Central Park West that houses more shrinks than the entire state of Montana. Death loves her children equally, all her pretty ones.

Hamlet, with Yorick's skull in hand: "Where be your gibes now? your gambols? your songs? your flashes of merriment, that were wont to set the table on a roar?"
Laughter is the father of beauty.

Commentary: As it turns out, my commentary is in journal form. The invitation to contribute to this book set me to musing about journals, which are sometimes—certainly in this case—an inky form of "thinking out loud." Dingbats divide my commentary-in-journal-form from some journal-in-journal-form.

"Where do you get your ideas from?" a poet gets asked, and all too seldom answers, "From other people." The notion that everything is *fatta in casa* is a widely tolerated fiction and may be the equivalent in creative life to the genial falsehood that all successful Ph.D. candidates have performed original scholarship.
From books, from other people, from every opportunism I can think of.

⁞

A reason to keep a journal is to stumble upon scraps long after one first meets them in their own contexts. It's easier to wonder, "Now, what could I make from that?" if one can no longer remember very precisely what someone else had made from it.
And a journal encourages scrappiness. Things needn't be finished, just stored, the way one might "store" a five-dollar bill in a trouser pocket in the closet for two weeks only to discover it smugly the next time the trousers get worn.

⁞

And *idea* is too big a word. It's not scrappy enough. An idea might lead to another, and thence to the exposition of an argument, and from there to the discovery of an intellectual pattern, and thence to an article, which might, of course, be expanded to a book. Next thing you know you've got a specialty, and you're the helpless owner of a career. "Sweet Baby Jesus," you'll be muttering to yourself, "if only I had a really good, small, selective scrap collection."

❧

Some writers keep their journals, or notebooks, the way a cook might tend a good strain of yeast or mother-of-vinegar. Roethke's notebooks, in David Wagoner's beautifully edited version of them, *Straw for the Fire,* were used that way. Apparently, he'd weed them each year, throwing out what no longer sparked. A few entries survived a dozen or more such cullings before Roethke put them to some use we can identify from his poems.

Roethke's was not a "scrapbook," with its hope to preserve something of the past, but a collection of scraps that yearn to be changed from their illusory current form into something else, something future. They're not to be kept but burned.

❧

If the hope a writer has for such scraps is that they might be changed, as fire converts matter to energy, we could imagine a kind of negative journal, a blank space into which no scraps are placed for fear that the shape those scraps are now in—or maybe we should say that those scraps *are* their shape?—will prove an obstruction to their conversion. They're deliberately forgotten, consigned to the unconscious for their slow, unwatched reformation. They do their work like leaf mold on the forest floor.

Then the bright, unmarred sheet of paper, which might otherwise become part of a journal, represents the future's blinding glare of potential.

❧

Elle vous suit partout. One of Byron's seals bore this motto, an incised, one-sentence journal entry. Does it describe a curse? A comfort? Why choose?

❧

Some writers don't need journals because they have waste-baskets.

❧

A morally sentimental 1968 rhyme: *Nazi/ROTC.*

❧

Is it more interesting to distinguish between different levels of evil than between different levels of good, or just easier?

As a boy, I thought "good" was monolithic, and so I remember vividly the first time I heard the phrase *too kind*. Who spoke of whom? Where? When? I don't remember. But the monolith began to crumble. Some loose pebbles, some rocks, next boulders, and then an avalanche.

❧

White southern women: "She's too kind."
Urban black boys: "He's bad."

❧

Irony is not a defense against emotion. It's an emotion about the relationship between words and emotion.

❧

But, then, emotion is a poor defense against irony.

❧

German food critic: "The wurst is full of passionate intensity."

❧

Of course it's a dumb joke. Are jokes about being smart? Are smart jokes about being dumb?

❧

Sebastian has asked me to give—to reinvent—one of the traditional blessings for his wedding to Ali.

I've who've blessed my marriages with divorce as a man shoots a broken-legged horse.

An uncouplet.

❧

I get number 7, which lists the ten shades of joy. A thrilling phrase, *ten shades of joy,* but how dull they turn out to be, striding up the ramp in pairs not to the Ark but to the Love Boat:

bridegroom and bride
mirth and exultation
pleasure and delight
love and fellowship
peace and friendship.

The problem, of course, may lie somewhat in the translation. They make redundant couples, like legal phrases:

intents and purposes
will and testament.

Of course, marriage and contract law are themselves a couple. But where's the breathlessness, the giddiness, the risk, the thrill and terror, of vowmaking? Eclipsed by all those abstract nouns.

છે.

Reinvent traditional ceremonies, and Who may wind up absent? The deity formerly known as Yahweh.

છે.

But here's the recurring problem poets face. The forms bristle with rust. Throw them wholly out, and you've asked yourself to start from prose and make a poem. But, if you're not suspicious of them and intelligently combative, they'll write your poem not for you but instead of you.

The purpose of the forms is to raise talk above babble, and the purpose of "talk" is to tether the severities of the forms to the mess of emotional life. It's a two-party system, and each party needs a loyal opposition.

છે.

Wouldn't it be easy to scrawl a journal entry in which I describe the relationship between the forms and talk as a mixed marriage, which would suggest why I, a deracinated WASP, will give the seventh blessing at a Jewish wedding?

Yes, as Nixon said, but it would be wrong.

Only a very great writer, Nabokov said in a related context, could resist such a temptation.

Well, then, I won't do it.

૨ૂ

The forms represent their own history, and the talk represents this singular instance in the history.

૨ૂ

The poem will be ten stanzas, of course, of ten lines each. Pentameter, natch. Perhaps each stanza might conclude with a couplet as an instance of knot tying. "Ten Shades of Joy."

Mingus at the Showplace

Interview with Sascha Feinstein

Throughout your career you've written about a number of astonishing jazz musicians, including John Coltrane, Coleman Hawkins, Lester Young, Bud Powell, Ben Webster, and Sidney Bechet. I'd like to talk this afternoon about your recent poems for the bassist Charles Mingus and your visits in 1960 to the Showplace, which featured Mingus's Jazz Workshop for half of that year. Nat Hentoff said that he inevitably brought friends visiting New York to the Showplace because at that time "there was no other experience in jazz at all like it."

Various accounts of what the business arrangements were have by now attached themselves to this legendary gig, but Mingus was in effect guaranteed a six-month stint at the Showplace. He was not just the entertainment but also the artist-in-residence. The group expanded its repertoire not in someone's loft or in a rented rehearsal space but in front of an audience every night. It allowed the audience a look at Mingus's terrific willfulness. He could gather and focus enormous vitality and purpose when he could arrange not to be distracted by his own personality.

I agree with Hentoff. The Jazz Workshop was unique in jazz at the time. And not just unique in format but in the daring and quality of the music. It was also unique in that it was truly a group enterprise and at the same time driven by dictatorial Mingus. How they managed this is hard to say, but here's one way to think about it.

Mingus's greatest influence as a composer, I've always thought—and it doesn't require a genius grasp of jazz history to know this—is, of course Ellington. Mingus learned something crucial to the enterprise of the Jazz Workshop from Ellington.

From *Brilliant Corners* 1, no. 1 (winter 1996).

He didn't learn it firsthand, for he didn't spend that much time around Ellington. But he understood deeply the way Ellington wrote some music not just for the trombone but for a particular trombonist in the band—Juan Tizol, let's say. He wrote for the individual style and tone and strengths of the Workshop members, and, like Ellington and Strayhorn, he sometimes incorporated phrases from his sidemen's improvisations into his written compositions. Mingus did his composing half at the piano at home and half on the stand.

No doubt Mingus was so hard on his pianists and fired so many of them, and often melodramatically and humiliatingly in public, because it was his teaching instrument—his classroom, in effect. He knew what he could hear from it, and when others wouldn't or couldn't hear likewise he forgot that they were not he, and thus the frustration he might otherwise have eaten he spat at them. The other musicians he wrote toward, but the pianists had to play toward him. And that was why the most unstable thing about the group was the identity of the pianist.

He went through so many piano players . . .

He used Horace Parlan. And he used people who sounded so unlike Horace Parlan you'd think they were from different planets.

Jaki Byard, Sir Roland Hanna, Kenny Drew, Paul Bley, Sy Johnson . . .

Nico Bunick, Tommy Flanagan. . . . The remarkable combination of tightness and exaltation that marks the *The Complete Candid Recordings of Charles Mingus* was built during that stay at the Showplace. Of course, Hentoff supervised (or is the right word *abetted?*) the *Candid Recordings* and thus speaks of those days with special authority. Mingus would often stop the band during a number to work on some detail or other. The sessions were not nightclub "entertainment" but more like a master class at Juillard.

A lot of stuff got reworked on the stand and not written down. It was only going to get written down after the fact or not at all. The famous debacles concerning the copyists for the Town Hall concert suggest that "not at all" was the correct answer. Mingus fulminated at copyists for not getting down what was only in his head. This dynamic duplicates with depressing neatness his relationship to his pianists.

You never knew if Danny Richmond, who was having smack problems in those years, was going to show up shivering like a cymbal or in fine form. Every so often he was so close to being on the nod it was like going back fifteen years in jazz and drug history, or so I imagined, for I was too young to know firsthand. But Mingus never let Richmond go. I've always thought some temperamental fit between Mingus and Richmond was the emotional glue of that group, which was built from the rhythm section up in a way that's not true of any other jazz organization except Basie's early band and maybe the Modern Jazz Quartet. No matter what a pain in the ass Richmond might be—and Mingus showed his discontent now and then—he knew not to get rid of him. Richmond's might well have been a broken career with any other leader.

I wasn't living in New York in those years and went into the city on weekends when I could, so I never sat in the Showplace three or four nights in a row listening to the group work its way slowly through the same piece. But from weekend to weekend you could hear the pieces evolve and the repertory grow. It was like watching time-lapse photography.

But you were there a lot.

I was there a lot.

And this was when you were seventeen years old, right?

Yes. I turned eighteen in November 1960.

Why did it take you thirty-five years to digest this experience and write about it?

I don't know why it took me so long to understand it. I knew in some visceral way I was witnessing a genius at work. I think most geniuses are monsters of a sort, but there's a difference between a pure monster—a loathsome thing—and a genius tinged by his gift with monstrosity. Perhaps I was scared as well as excited by the intensity and difficulty of what happened at the Showplace.

No doubt in some way that was adolescently romantic, but not therefore necessarily false, I realized that artists, black people, and others marginalized by mainstream American culture were dramatizing my possible lives far more accurately than mainstream American culture could. That would explain both the fear and the excitement.

I wasn't one of those white kids who thought he was secretly black. The gap between whites and blacks seemed to me immense and tragic. Norman Mailer's essay "The White Negro" was in the air in those days, but it seemed to me a kind of hipster's wet dream. I thought, "Hang out with some nonliterary blacks for a few days, Norman, and learn how full you are of shit." [*Laughs.*]

Also, Mingus's music was dense and layered, at the same time it was immediately exciting. It took a while to understand how complex and sophisticated it was, for all its emotional force. The combination of the two is unusual in art, though there's no self-evident reason why one must be achieved at the cost of the other, and work in which the two cohabit usually takes a while for partial understandings of it to grow full.

The more interesting our experience is, the more slowly it submits to understanding. That tenacity may be our first sign of how interesting a particular body of experience is.

Recently someone asked me when it first occurred to me to translate Horace (I've been working on his satires the last couple of years), and I remember thinking in my late twenties, not knowing if it meant anything more than bravado, "I'll translate Horace one day, when I'm older and more skillful." I started in my early fifties. I guess I'm a slow study! [*Laughs.*]

❧

A few years ago you told me that your poem "Mingus at The Showplace" was 98 percent autobiographical, and I love that moment when this seventeen-year-old speaker, "casting beer money from a thin reel of ones," shows Mingus his poem based on what he considers "miserable" experience. Did you show Mingus the poem because Mingus himself was interested in poetry?

Mingus was said to be interested in poetry, and Al Young, who was around Mingus in those years . . . Al and I must have spent some nights in the same room.

He was there at the same time.

But neither of us remembers that, of course. We met years later. Well, given the narcissism one has at that age, it would be a wonder if I remembered anyone else being there.

Al has a wonderful reflection on the Showplace in his Mingus/Mingus *book, written with Janet Coleman.*

Yes, I like the book a lot. I've talked to Al about Mingus and his interest in poetry. I think Al's memory may be more trust-worthy than mine, in this sense: once I've transformed some memories by writing about them, the resulting poems tend to shadow the originating memories. I think that for Al the source and the poems coexist more equably. And Mingus certainly respected poets and poetry, as remarks in liner notes, the *Village Voice*, and elsewhere in that period suggested. I don't know how avid a reader of poetry he was. I think he cared about it some, quite genuinely, and if he got a reputation for caring about it more than he really did he wasn't about to offer a public correction of that misconception.

Not a great reader, perhaps, but poetry crept into several of his records—The Clown, *for example—and he played on the Langston Hughes date* [Weary Blues].

Yes, and not perfunctorily either. He really showed up for that one. That's the kind of gig some musicians would phone in.

Sure. Hughes noticed it, too, and said he preferred the session with Mingus.

Of course, the poets are so thrilled to have the musicians there they often don't care if the musicians play anything interesting or not.

That's often true. What do you think of Mingus's autobiography, Beneath the Underdog? *That's a very complex question, I realize.*

Well, let's dispose of the accuracy question right off and assume that the truth of this autobiography is not historical but emotional truth. If you can read it that way, it's very moving. I love Mingus's descriptions of his early years as an acolyte bassist in L.A. and of how grateful he was to his teachers and anyone with skill who gave him any time at all. We're both teachers and know how rare gratitude can be. [*Laughs.*]

I love about the jazz tradition the way musicians tip their hats and pay their dues. By contrast, poets tend to act as if they'd discovered their abilities under a cabbage. Thanks are important.

They're a necessity.

Oh yeah. Absolutely. There was no schoolhouse for this class, so names have to be named.

The early part of Mingus's book raises the fewest questions of truthfulness, chronological accuracy, etc. I find his account of his personal and musical boyhood very moving. It has some of the same wacko confidence that [James Joyce's] *A Portrait of the*

Artist as a Young Man has, as if to say, "I'm going to make this character so interesting that you won't mind spending all this time on his earliest years." There's less grandiosity and myth-making here than anywhere else in the book, but still there's a sense that his teachers were not only fine teachers and musicians but important the way the guy who tutored Alexander the Great was important. Alexander doubtless thought that was the most important thing his tutor ever did.

Perhaps the hardest thing for Mingus to come to terms with, and the aspect of his book to which my proposition that an emotional truth is captured by laying waste to other kinds of truth, is the impact of race on jazz in Mingus's world. He had a Martin Luther King side to him and a Malcolm X side, and they never got along. They're at war, contesting for the microphone, whenever the subject comes up in the book, as it crucially must come up early and often. He lived with white women. He hired Jimmy Knepper to play trombone for him because he thought Knepper the best available trombonist even if Knepper was a honky. He kept exciting the conflict.

To compare and contrast, let's think of Art Blakey, who just hired hip and talented young black musicians and saved himself all the drama.

Mingus kept making decisions—erotic decisions, sideman decisions, recording contract decisions—that kept the problem on his plate, and then his contesting instincts on the matter made grandiloquent and "false" reactions, like Siamese twins turned on one another. One thought himself a Jeffersonian and the other a bilious, broken-hearted black nationalist. The other thought his counterpart a Tom and himself a clear-eyed racial realist.

Both "Mingus at The Showplace" and "Mingus at The Half Note" conclude with the image of the music pushing forward: the first ending, "and the band played on"; the second, "he kick-starts the band: / One, two, one two three four." There are other striking similarities. Do you see these as variations on a theme? Do you see why I would think that?

Yeah, I do. They're both apparently anecdotal pieces, but both end with Mingus's will and urgency in command. I wanted to register my own naïveté and voyeurism. I wanted to admit, without making a big deal of it, that the person who goes to hear these things does so for love of the music but also for complicated reasons of his own—thus the passage about "the excited calm / of the hip in congregation" and my description of myself with "big ears like a puppy." I wanted to register what a rube I was and the pleasure I took in being someplace cool without switching the ardor of the poem from Mingus—a shot of the ears in silhouette, with the focus not on the foregrounded ears but on Mingus. [*Chuckles.*] After writing them was perhaps when I first noticed that the poems knew something I hadn't, except by writing the poems, of course: the rhythmic drive of the music and Mingus's willfulness are nearly identical in the poems. I had to know that in order to write the poems, one might say, but I think it's truer to say I had to write the poems to know that.

While I was working on *Time & Money,* I kept thinking there should be two more Mingus poems—one about him after his death (what happens to the dynasty) and one about his death and the way it became instantly mythologized. I couldn't get the second one right, and then the deadline for adding anything to the manuscript passed. Within a week I was able to get that poem, too.

Of course!

It will follow in my next book. It's a poem about the last photograph of Mingus, which appears in the biography of Mingus by—what's his name?

Priestly.

Right, Brian Priestly, who wrote that "critical" biography, using the word critical fairly loosely. You know the photo, and I think you've heard that poem, haven't you?

Yes. It's a terrific piece, as is the third Mingus poem that appeared in Time & Money, *"Mingus in Diaspora." That's not nearly as anecdotal as the other two in the book. What's the history behind that poem?*

Two things I can think of.

One is the phrase from Auden's elegy for Yeats: "He became his admirers." That's the literal diaspora, the scattering: the homeland, in this case the body, is gone and irretrievable.

The other is the long process of accumulating expertise. Let's imagine it as an emotional and intellectual version of aerobic gain—the way repeated exercise forms new tributaries to the circulatory system. An artist spends years ramifying these new passages, and then at death they're gone, winked out, absolutely ceased. How do artists make complex and accurate decisions fast and intuitively? How do musicians teach themselves to improvise? How do chess players look at the board and sense that they're in dire trouble in the upper left corner of the board six moves from now? They provide a kind of alert flexibility for themselves the way a pond "makes" algae. If you die comparatively young, as Mingus did, this beautiful construction, not the work itself but the attention that made the work possible, dies early, too.

Well, he lived to be fifty-six, older than many of his contemporaries, but still he died far too young.

There are players from his era still building—Flanagan, Kenny Barron. . . .

Barron actually played at the Showplace with Mingus. He must have been remarkably young. [Note: Kenny Barron was born in 1943!]

I was surprised by the apocryphal stories that attached themselves to Mingus's death, such as the one that fifty-six whales beached themselves in Baja on that day.

But the "Diaspora" poem has nothing anecdotal in it, and it mourns the winking out of Mingus's hard-won expertise. I even give Mingus's music a possibly longer period of incubation than his own life span by bringing his bass and its maker into the poem.

Mingus had an old bass and a new bass. Maybe sequentially, but I suspect he had them together. He referred to the one in his hands as "The Bass," but there were two of them—two halves of a whole personality, perhaps. It always seemed right to me he would have a Jekyll and Hyde bass. [*Laughs.*]

Mingus remains such a mythic figure, as are several jazz musicians from the 1950s and 1960s, and, like many poets, you have focused your jazz poems on those musicians. I know that you're not locked in time, that you often go downtown to hear contemporary players—but why do you keep returning to the past?

I think the period in jazz history that has the most emotional voltage for a person is that period when he fell in love with the music. To return to the music recapitulates the beginning of a grand affair.

Maybe, but—

Of course, I think it's one of the crucial periods of jazz history.

It is.

And it's coincidental that I happen to have begun listening attentively to the music then. It was a period so rich and complex, so difficult socially and racially, that after those years spent themselves jazz entered some doldrums. Much dull stuff. Jazz in New York, if New York is still an accurate jazz microcosm, and I think it is, has some of the health now it had in those years but not the same sense of reckless and unstoppable growth. In the halcyon years, if you were trying to keep up, you might need to go to two or even three clubs a night. Not now: there's usually one clearly stellar attraction a week.

One reason that those great years lost their momentum was an increasing polarization of musicians along racial lines, stylistic lines, etc. The network grew smaller, there was less cross-pollination, and jazz broke up for a while into small islands of the saved, always a dreadful situation.

I remember going to hear Coltrane and Dolphy, and the act they alternated sets with was Stan Getz.

No kidding?

They were coming from different places but listened to one another. But soon you heard people say things like, "I can't learn anything from anyone who's not into free jazz."

Getz and Dolphy were on nearly opposite ends of some bar graph or other, but they were both great musicians and so listened to one another. Coltrane tended always to listen for some cloud nobody else knew the location of, but Dolphy and Getz each listened carefully to something he had no inclination to play.

And Coltrane once said, "We'd all play like Getz if we could." It's not a compliment without a faintly serrated edge, but I think he meant it in some generous way, too.

❧

One of the reasons I was eager to talk to you about these Mingus poems is that this seems to be the first time in your career when you have, at least publicly, presented a series of poems about the same figure in jazz. It's not as though you couldn't have. I mean, you've written about some stunningly inspirational figures, and I imagine there are a number of Lester [Young] poems in you. But what was it about Mingus that inspired this series?

I had the most complicated relationship to Mingus. I set that up for myself rather deliberately. Call it hero worship, call it role model. . . . I picked him as a tutelary figure.

What would it be like to take a complicated and obsessive project and say to yourself, "It doesn't matter that this seems foolish to everyone else and often to me. It's important. I'm going to do it. I'm willing to waste my breath, my energy, my love on it."

Of course, I was dimly preparing myself for something and didn't want to say very clearly to myself what it might be. For one reason, I didn't know. For another, it would have been a little scary to say to myself, "Well, you're probably longing for some impossible project yourself, you fool, and don't want to look like an idiot."

Self-knowledge might be fine, but it could come later, as Saint Augustine said about chastity. [*Laughs.*]

I have certain dopey identifications with Lester Young, it's true. There's a combination in Young of strong emotion, not so much concealed as released by diffidence, irony, and sweetness of tone, that doesn't sound far off from certain textures in my poems, unless my ear is off.

No, you're absolutely right.

I'm a little more angular and boppy, being a child of a later age. But a sense of fellow feeling is strong. Young went into hiding more than Mingus's temperament would have permitted him. Possibly Mingus is a better tutelary figure for a younger writer, who needs the courage of his brashness and anger. Maybe, then, Young would serve a writer in his later years, when all the important confrontations are internal.

These are also, of course, two black styles, like Richard Wright's on the one hand and Ralph Ellison's on the other, and as a white man I'm somewhat to the side of that. But only somewhat. One point of the music and of poetry is that we can imagine what it means to be each other and that we'll be made by that empathy, well, if not free, then more human and more nearly whole.

I didn't, of course, set out to write about Mingus in some political way or as an instance of how a white boy starts to think seriously about race in American life or about the relationship between the intuitive and emotional to voracious will—sometimes Mingus seemed to be three hundred pounds of frontal lobe. But I wound up having to think about all those things and whatever else I could get into the poems. He's just so large that I think one poem wouldn't do it.

The Pleasure of Experience, the Experience of Pleasure

Interview with Peter Davison

You have done a lot of translation, from Latin, Greek, French, Hebrew. What do you learn from the poets of other languages?

There's always a gap between the two languages, between the time at which the original was written and the time when the translation was done, between what the translator can feel and what the translator can bring across. It's possible to write poems in French that can't be written in English. Each language knows a part of reality. For whatever reasons, certain parts of reality are specific to certain languages. We learn what it would have been like to have been born into another language.

What have you specifically learned from Horace, from Martial?

Horace and Martial are interested in how humans interact. What matters to these poets is what is most vivid to us and what energizes us most on a daily basis—a life defined by the ways in which humans are social animals, the ways in which we suffer from being social animals. From Martial I learned foremost how important it is to find ways to be angry with human folly and failure and to be forgiving of it at the same time, because you know when your turn to be riddled with folly comes around that you'll do a great job.

From Horace I learned that pleasure in itself and friendship in itself are valuable subjects, period. They don't need to be compared to anything. You don't need to go through the masquerade of the Renaissance, for example, in which romantic love is important because it imitates divine love. Love is important on its own terms and because of its own experience, and

From the *Atlantic Unbound* (October 1997).

159

that's an end to it. Horace's bemusement with the elaborate construction and parody (at the same time) of his own persona is a spectacle. Horace's way of understanding what it means to be Horace is so much more complicated and richer than most of what our culture makes available to us that it's tonic.

Could your poetry be described as the poetry of experience? In what sense?

Well, it's certainly not the poetry of innocence. What happens to us is, I suppose, interesting because it happens to us? No, actually I don't think that. Life happens to us whether we have the good sense to be interested in the way it happens to us or not. That's what it means to be alive. Paying attention to it and trying to figure out what it does and doesn't mean (and what's wrong with seeking for meaning in experience?)—these are opportunities. I would like to think that in my poems I am as interested in and bemused by and willing to follow and question simultaneously those opportunities as I am while I'm being a civilian—while I'm just being alive without the slightest thought that a poet lives his or her life differently than somebody else with another vocation.

Your poems show a good deal of admiration for Freud. In what sense?

Well, I'm unqualified to admire Freud as a clinician. I admire Freud as a writer, as someone who's interested in the making of meaning, the meaning of meaning, the ways in which the idea of meaning doesn't make sense. He's interested in how dreams are made, how jokes are made. He's interested in the "psychopathology of everyday life"—a beautiful title! Though if it happens to us all the while perhaps it deserves a less medical term than *psychopathology*. There's much else. Many of Freud's papers and individual essays and other books are glorious. We live in a period when a great deal of Freud-bashing is fashionable: the feminists want at him; the deconstructionists want at him; anybody who has a specific theoretical axe to grind wants at him. But Freud is somebody fascinated and appalled by the power of the human imagination to deceive itself, to save itself from peril, to hide from itself exactly what it needs to save itself, to hide from itself exactly what would destroy it—all of these things seem to me great imaginative curiosities, and I love and admire Freud for having them.

I've lived in a century much determined by Freud's vocabulary and Freud's curiosities. I suppose I have ambivalent feelings toward him, the way we have ambivalent feelings toward any power that controls us in ways we don't fully understand. I admire his courage, his nuttiness, his obsessions. I like particularly his moments when he admits he doesn't know what the hell he is doing, and I love those moments when he's crazedly certain what he's doing, some of which have held up far less well than others. Though I certainly don't have fluent German and am not in a position to judge him as a prose stylist in German, I do feel that I have some ability to judge him as a writer, as a maker and shaper of tales. He is a great exemplary figure, and I wish that those people who are so eager to diminish his achievement would take the trouble to go back and reread him before they continue on their quest.

A friend of yours once told me that you rather relished the attitude of sprezzatura, as the Italians call it—an air of faint disdain toward your own importance. True?

By and large, true. I don't think my life story is interesting because it happened to me. A story that's interesting because it happened to the person it happened to is by definition unlikely to be interesting to a second party. I'm not a particularly autobiographical poet. There are circumstances and urges and emotions and quandaries and recurring problems that of course come through my work. I'm an autobiographical writer, therefore, to the extent that no writer can avoid being autobiographical, but I'm not a systematic and relentlessly autobiographical poet to the extent that, say, James Merrill was. Merrill had perhaps a more interesting and exemplary story to tell. I am to some extent bored by the story of my own life, with its repetitions, its recurrence of the same problems, its long dawdle periods, its spikes of embarrassing melodrama. That doesn't mean that I've ignored it when my life required me to write about it, rather than the other way around—that is, when my life as a writer offered me the opportunity to write about my life. Furthermore, I like to think that the attention I have to pay to the world is acute and large; but, in fact, while you're concentrating on being, you're probably seeing rather blurrily. The idea that I would spend much of my life paying attention to the details of my own life, rather than trying to understand what it would feel like to be someone else, someone different, someone born in a different body, born as a member of a different sex, born in a different time or a different place—the curiosity you can spend on being yourself in spades rather than being someone else—well, it's clear that I've consistently preferred the former to the latter.

Your poems concern themselves a lot with pleasure—music, wine, love, language—yet with a difference.

I don't think there's been nearly as large a body of poetry that concerns itself with pleasure as there has been that concerns itself with other emotions—despair, sexual jealousy, terrible intrafamilial battles, etc. Of course, the circumstance under which the poet chooses to pay attention to one thing rather than another never means that he or she believes it is more important. You don't take on subject matter because of an objective sense that one sort of subject matter is more important than something else. You take on what you can handle, what you can transform, what you can make your own, what you can make explicable and clear to somebody else, the reader who might stumble across the poem and recognize his or her life in that cloudy mirror.

What would the "difference" that your question suggests mean? I hope it means that I have been willing to consider the possibility that pleasure in itself, with regard for it as something that lessens our suffering, offers a consolation, a relief—I wanted to be able to avoid a vocabulary that insists on the secondariness or the tertiariness of pleasure. I would like to say that one of the primary reasons for being alive is to experience the pleasure of being alive. I would like to write as if it were a given to rise and look out the window on a particularly beautiful light on a summer morning or on one of those winter mornings when snow has fallen and made the whole of New York City quiet, or you name your favorite such sight. To write of the experience of these things without any instinct to translate them into a relationship to humanism or God or philosophy or any idea but simply because these impressions or perceptions were part of what it means to be human and maybe because they are as close as we come to understanding the relationship of the human to the divine. That would be fine. I would love to be able to do that. Pleasure is in itself and by itself valuable and important.

Of course, a perception is, to someone who is by habit a writer, first of interest in itself, but then it's interesting because it's very hard to describe, and the job of a writer is to describe it. If there was ever a moment (and I don't know for a writer that there is) when that perception existed independent of that writer's deep investment in language, the question of translating that perception from the five senses to what for any writer is the sixth sense—language—immediately becomes the valuable, possible, infernal, never-perfect-enough, and absolutely fascinating next work-to-be-done.

Can you tell me a little about "Dire Cure" [Atlantic *(October 1997)]?*

I was married to a woman who got a disastrous cancer. It took her over a year of treatment to know whether she was going to be able to fend it off. It took her a couple of years after that to begin to think that it might stay away. She is, I'm happy to be able to report, still in good health, and the cancer, a particularly aggressive one, has shown no signs of coming back.

Almost everybody invites you to think about your experience in terms that are not helpful. People describe you as the Caregiver or the Helpmeet. None of the categories make any sense. People aren't imposing dopey categories on you out of malice; they don't know better. I wouldn't have known better in their place. I wouldn't have known a vocabulary even for talking about the subject. One of the reasons you wind up writing a poem is not because cancer is such great material for a poem; I think it's very intractable material for a poem. Material that has a great deal of melodrama built into it—murder, cancer, rape, child molestation—once you mention the subject, everybody knows the poem. The child molestation poem will have footsteps, for example. The footsteps are like mood music in a horror movie or a gothic novel. The problem is to write a poem on child molestation in which footsteps don't occur—as, for example, in Linda Gregerson's good poem on the subject ["For the Taking," *Atlantic* (November 1993)]. That's hard work.

It's not easy to write a poem on these subjects. I didn't write a poem because I thought it would be useful material. On the contrary: I noticed all the way through that neither I nor anybody else has much of a vocabulary for talking about my experience or talking about Pat's experience (to the extent that I could guess what that was or hear her tell me).

Would you call it an act of witness?

Yes, it's an act of witness, but I needed to write the poem to invent a vocabulary, because it's a matter of pride for me not to be linguistically inadequate. We are all rendered mute and stupid by our experience from time to time, but the point of being a poet is that you have redress. I felt particularly challenged in this instance. It seemed to me a matter of pride—I hope I don't mean puffed-up pride but the pride that a good cook takes in knowing how to save a curdling sauce. It was also an act of trying to rescue an important part of human experience from imaginative failures and thinness of vocabulary and failures of empathy. You can't give up to the forces of silence. They mean us harm.

You have served on the National Endowment for the Arts, the Poetry Society of America, and numerous other arts agencies and associations. Do you regard these as the necessary chores of a good citizen?

I've had a lucky poetry life. I've never had to carry one of my manuscripts from publisher to publisher, suffering many disappointing rejections and finally stumbling upon a solution for publishing a particular book that I was not happy with. Instead, for most of my life I've had one excellent editor, and, accurately or not, the official world of poetry has offered me a fellowship here, an award there. If you have dined well, you should do the dishes. Yes, these are the chores of a good citizen. On the other hand, I don't want to sound selfless. There's something I learned from being president of the Poetry Society or literature chair of the National Endowment for the Arts. I learned how the poetry world worked in terms of finances, publicity. I learned more about the intersection between the world of poetry and the world of the imagination and the world of ordinary life, business, journalism, publicity, rentin' the hall, gettin' the crowd out—I learned more about that than perhaps I was temperamentally prepared to learn any other way. In some cases I learned that I had the worst possible temperament for fund-raising. I had no idea how to ask people for money. The fund-raising gene had just been omitted from my DNA. I was wired wrong at the factory, and there was nothing to be done to remedy this. There were things I would never be able to do. I learned other things I didn't know I knew; I learned some lacks in myself. I don't want it to appear that all of it was good citizenship and I gained nothing from it.

The poetry world is very unfair. There are many talented people who have never been, and will never be, sufficiently rewarded for the value of the work they have done. There is something to be said for making sure that people who care about poetry, who operate all its readings, all its endless conferences, all the various dates and occasions that call people who care about poetry together—it's important that there be mechanisms whereby these people can be known to one another and that these opportunities be made available. We live in a big country. It's not Belgium, where all the poets in the country can get on trains and be in Brussels in half an hour. There are lots of good American poets who are doing what they do in comparative isolation from one another. Keeping a network of information and opportunity and emotional support, to the extent that that can be offered, is an act of corporal mercy, and it needs to be done. There are people out there with a longing to find a relationship between their emotional life and language and the way they live in and understand their world. Anything we can do that accidentally makes that easier for anyone is a human good and needs to be done.

Are there guardians at the door, and are they the right ones?

The situation of the arts is two-faced. One face is the face of equal opportunity. Everybody gets a try: equal opportunity. To that face there should be no guardian at the door—it's open admissions. The other face is the face that deals not with opportunity and hope but with the quality of the actual work produced and the extremely high standards that are required to sort out the very most enduring and emotionally useful work from the next level down and the many other levels below that. That doesn't require a guardian. It requires time, which sorts these things out, cruelly, but with a terrible efficiency.

Both faces are required, particularly for an American. We must try to live up to the glorious rhetoric of the founding fathers and mothers of our country and say, Listen, everybody gets a shot at this, nobody is excluded from it, there's nobody at the door. Later on, time is at the door, erosion is at the door, forgetfulness is at the door, oblivion is at the door. These are worse than any three-headed dog ever.

Is there anything else you want to talk about?

Well, I was on the edge of saying something earlier about the extent to which poetry is subject to pressures from the larger culture. We treat poetry as though we were all living in an orchid plantation—in one of the greenhouses, too. But in fact the general weather infects us, and, when people complain, as is so fashionable to do, about the supposedly small audience of poetry and by that the perilous health of poetry, I never find that I recognize the world they are talking about. They are talking about a world in which marketing is much more important to them than it is to me. I'm thinking about Dana Gioia's piece ("Can Poetry Matter?" *Atlantic* [May 1991]), which is largely about marketing. We get the high modernist grumpiness about the "poorly educated and highly absent audience." As Sol Hurok (or was it Yogi Berra?) said, "If they want to stay away in droves, you can't stop them." Berating the audience is silly.

We forget that 150 years ago what you did at night in a house in the Midwest (where I grew up) was to sit around the piano or read. Now I have in my living room extraordinary performances in a wide range of music, the sort of stuff that a hundred years ago you couldn't hear unless you lived in a major city and had a lot of disposable income. There's interesting stuff on television. I live in a city famous for its ability to distract its citizens with interesting cultural and entertainment events. The competition for the attention of people who pay some attention to poetry, and might pay more, is at an unprecedented level in human history.

I don't think that anyone can look around and see Adrienne Rich and Philip Levine and W. S. Merwin and Yusef Komunyakaa and Josephine Jacobsen and say that American poetry is not doing very well. Two-thirds of the poets who interest me in the generation younger than I am are women. These are the people who have been absent from the table for the last couple of generations, and it was a scandal. Now poets are at the table from all over the place. I think American poetry is very healthy. I don't understand what it is that gives people pleasure in pronouncing it ill or prematurely dead, but I wish they'd stop. However it is we're bumbling along, we're doing okay. Let's have less talk about what can be done for the patient. Most of those pieces are self-serving. They are written by a doctor who has a better technology, and they are essentially self-serving pieces. Let the health of poetry go along in its own ad hoc way, because, whatever we're not doing, it's good for us.

The Complaint

I don't complain that he has misrepresented me, for the impersonation is skillful. Slander is scarcely the issue: on balance he has made me seem both a livelier and better person than I fear I am.

People who make the mistake that I am he expect an ironic skepticism, a bruised worldliness, and maybe, like a caption you wouldn't have thought a picture needed until an exact one got supplied, an apt little tag phrase, maybe in Latin. He is, people say, witty and also smart. I feel like a widower's bride being told of her brilliant predecessor, and I fill with formless murk.

The people who tell me these things while I stand stiffly mute are not the ones to whom I seem both a livelier and better person than I really am, needless to say.

People I've never met make that mistake, and why would I have met them? Who stands behind a podium and theatrically extracts his reading glasses from a nifty leather case, rocks back on his heels and unreels some genial patter, and then reads, in that cigarette-rasped old-friends voice of his, a poem that the hipper members of the audience applaud by making small, barely but firmly audible, all-vowel noises, like gerbil orgasms? Who travels to the Rockefeller Foundation's Study and Conference Center on Lake Como to write for a month under a cantilevered Tizio lamp and then returns with droll instructions to find the best *gelati* in Bellagio? Mr. Travel on Other People's Money, that's who. Mr. Leisure of the Theory Class.

Well, I guess you can hear the resentment now. I'm the emotional one, wit be damned, and he's broken my heart. It wasn't always like this. In the beginning I wallowed in his attentions.

"Me?" I would think, fluttering at the mirror.

From *Antaeus*.

Then: "Me!"

Then, of course, I knew, or thought I knew, what he wanted. But now? Material? He's not an "autobiographical" writer. I often recognize my emotions, of course, in his poems. But they're shorn of the exact details and private references that made them mine. They have details and references he's made up, but those could be anyone's. And anyone's is drab.

That's why I resent him. OK, I'm very emotional and easily filled with formless murk, and sometimes I get weepy like this, I'm sorry. Yes, thank you. He's glib, he files his tongue before he brushes his teeth, and he's diligent as a dog. He hasn't called in two days.

He looks like me but happier.

I don't suppose this will matter to your investigation, but I stole the phrase *formless murk* from a rejected draft of one of his poems. *Stole* is perhaps the wrong word. He'd thrown it away. I didn't have to uncrumple any paper. It was in plain view. He owes me a lot.

What? That's not a hard question. Of course it's a domestic dispute. After all, which of the persons I mentioned is missing?

UNDER DISCUSSION
David Lehman, General Editor
Donald Hall, Founding Editor

Volumes in the Under Discussion series collect reviews and essays about individual poets. The series is concerned with contemporary American and English poets about whom the consensus has not yet been formed and the final vote has not been taken. Titles in the series include: